An In-Depth Commentary On
The Diseases of the Heart
And Their Cure

By Shaykh al-Islâm Ibn Taymiya

The Diseases of the Heart and their Cure by Shaykh al-Islâm Ibn Taymiya

Commentary: Dr Yaser Borhamy
Translation: Mohammad Elshinawy
Editor: AbdelMinem Mustafa
Cover Design: Ifrah Inam, Ifrah Art & Design (@ifrahart)
1. Spirituality 2. Islam 3. Self Help 4. Metaphysical
First Edition
Printed in USA

Table of Contents

An In-Depth Commentary On
The Diseases of the Heart
And Their Cure

By Shaykh al-Islâm Ibn Taymiya

In the name of Allah, the Most Merciful, the Bestower of Mercy

Translator's Foreword

مَّا يَفْتَحِ اللَّهُ لِلنَّاسِ مِن رَّحْمَةٍ فَلَا مُمْسِكَ لَهَا ۖ وَمَا يُمْسِكْ فَلَا مُرْسِلَ لَهُ مِن بَعْدِهِ

**Whatever mercy Allah grants, none can withhold it, and whatever He withholds -
none can release it after Him.** [Surat Fâṭir (35): 2]

Every Muslim lives with the conviction that Allah, the Most Merciful, sent His final Messenger 🕊 as a mercy to all the worlds. Many a times, though, we conceptually limit that Prophetic mercy to merely the kind treatment of others. In reality, though, of the greatest manifestations of this divine mercy is the flawless revelation that fine-tuned much of what we innately know, or have come to understand through empiricism, about ourselves as human beings and how we function.

The mechanics of human nature, if you will, was vividly gifted to us through revelation to facilitate both our physical and spiritual wellbeing. Certainly, being informed by Allah that the flesh of swine is harmful, 1400 years before medical practitioners could explain why, is a splendid gift that saves countless lives. However, being informed about the intricacies of the heart and soul is a far greater bounty, for it deals with the unseen which tangible research can never fully grasp, and because so much more is contingent upon them being healthy than just lives. Rather, eternity is at stake, and the successful person is the one whom Allah allows to realize that this statement is not cliché, but in fact the ultimate reality.

Beloved students of knowledge, my brothers and sisters in faith, in your hands is a work I translated because I expect its original format, and the intention behind it, from both its author and commentator, will deem it beneficial on earth and acceptable in the heavens. It vividly carries its reader through the mechanics of the heart, its diseases, and the fountains that fuel its health. Consider its content carefully, for its words were chosen carefully, and teach it to the world, for they need it more than they know. May it be a means to purifying our hearts and lives, finally escaping our vices, safely journeying towards Allah, and properly standing before Him on the Last Day.

Finally, I cannot forget to thank Allah whose bounties are an unending rain in our lives, for making this possible in more ways than can be explained. And as our Prophet ﷺ taught us, we have not thanked Allah until we thank the people; a very special thanks to my parents whom I can never repay, to the scholars who are my access to the revelation, to Dr. Hatem al-Haj in particular for being the mentor of my life, and to my wife and children for patiently enduring the turbulent lifestyle of serving Islam. As well, I cannot forget Asif Siddiqui, Farah Khan, Abdel-Minem Mustafa, and Rihab Othman, for their valuable contributions to the production of this work. You have all been a burst of Allah's mercy in my life, and may Allah perfect for us the final installment of that mercy in the hereafter. Âmeen.

O Allah, if we are unable to reach Your mercy, Your mercy can surely reach us. O Allah, your mercy is wider than all things, and I am a thing, so accommodate me in Your mercy. O Allah, whatever is void of Your assistance will fail, and whatever is not for Your sake is a waste, so grant us a surge of support from above, guide our pens to correctness in what we write, and fasten our hearts upon sincerity throughout. Âmeen.

Mohammad Elshinawy

2nd of Ramadan, 1435H / 29th of June, 2014

In the name of Allah, the Most Merciful, the Grantor of Mercy
Commentator's Foreword

All praise is due to Allah, we thank Him, we seek His help, His guidance, His pleasure, and His forgiveness. We seek refuge with Allah from the evil [whispers] of our souls and the evil [consequences] of our actions. Whoever Allah guides, none can misguidance, and whoever Allah misguides, none can guide. We testify that none is worthy of worship except Allah, alone without a partner, and that Muhammad is His servant and Messenger.

يَا أَيُّهَا الَّذِينَ آمَنُوا اتَّقُوا اللَّهَ حَقَّ تُقَاتِهِ وَلَا تَمُوتُنَّ إِلَّا وَأَنتُم مُّسْلِمُونَ

O you who have believed, fear Allah as He should be feared and do not die except as Muslims [in submission to Him]. [Âl-'Imrân (3): 102]

يَا أَيُّهَا النَّاسُ اتَّقُوا رَبَّكُمُ الَّذِي خَلَقَكُم مِّن نَّفْسٍ وَاحِدَةٍ وَخَلَقَ مِنْهَا زَوْجَهَا وَبَثَّ مِنْهُمَا رِجَالًا كَثِيرًا وَنِسَاءً وَاتَّقُوا اللَّهَ الَّذِي تَسَاءَلُونَ بِهِ وَالْأَرْحَامَ إِنَّ اللَّهَ كَانَ عَلَيْكُمْ رَقِيبًا

O mankind, fear your Lord, who created you from one soul and created from it its mate and dispersed from both of them many men and women. And fear Allah, through whom you ask one another, and the wombs. Indeed Allah is ever, over you, an Observer. [an-Nisâ' (4): 1]

يَا أَيُّهَا الَّذِينَ آمَنُوا اتَّقُوا اللَّهَ وَقُولُوا قَوْلًا سَدِيدًا يُصْلِحْ لَكُمْ أَعْمَالَكُمْ وَيَغْفِرْ لَكُمْ ذُنُوبَكُمْ وَمَن يُطِعِ اللَّهَ وَرَسُولَهُ فَقَدْ فَازَ فَوْزًا عَظِيمًا

O you who have believed, fear Allah and speak words of appropriate justice. He will rectify for you your deeds, and forgive for you your sins, and whomever obeys Allah and His Messenger has certainly achieved the greatest achievement.

[al-Aḥzâb (33): 70-71]

I bear witness that the most truthful of speech is the Book of Allah, and the best of guidance is the guidance of Muhammad ﷺ, and that the worst of matters are the newly introduced matters [in the religion], for every newly introduced matter is a [reprehensible] innovation, and every innovation is a misguidance, and every misguidance is in the Hellfire.

A sound heart is the reason a person is saved in this world, and then in the hereafter when no wealth or children will benefit – save for someone who comes to Allah with a sound heart. Mujâhid and al-Ḥasan said, "A sound heart means [sound] from *shirk* (polytheism)." Sa'eed b. al-Musayyib said, "The healthy heart is the heart of the believer, because the heart of the disbeliever and hypocrite is diseased." Abu 'Uthmân an-Naysâboori said, "It refers to a heart that is sound from *bid'ah* (innovation) and content with the Sunnah (Prophetic example)." These reports from the righteous predecessors demonstrate a number of diseases which, if the heart is sound from them, the person is saved. These (*shirk*, disbelief, hypocrisy, and innovation) are simply the greatest of them. However, 'Ikrima mentioned that the statement of the Most High, **"…lest he whose heart is diseased become hopeful,"** [al-Ahzab (33): 32] was referring to the fornicators, adding by that the disease of forbidden lusts to our list.

We live an age where the trials of doubts and desires have become rampant and filled much of our hearts with diseases. Furthermore, the advising physicians have become so few, and those who use the effective remedy have become so rare. We have become direly in need of cleansing our hearts, purifying them of these diseases, and protecting them from what surrounds them. And we cannot think of anyone like Shaykh al-Islâm Ibn Taymiya (may Allah bestow mercy upon him) to clarify for us the reality of our ailments and the proper usage of the remedy, so that we may be cured by the Book of Allah (the Glorified and Exalted).

In this work, we chose to serve his blessed treatise, *The Diseases of the Hearts and their Cure*, by providing a bit of explanation and commentary for it. We ask Allah to benefit us with it in this world and the hereafter, and we ask Him (the Most High) to augment his reward, elevate his rank, forgive us and him and all the Muslims, allows us to die as Muslim, and to reunite us with the righteous. Âmeen.

Written by

Yâsir Borhamy

Commentator

The Diseases of the Hearts & their Cure

By Shaykh al-Islâm Ibn Taymiya

All praise is due to Allah. We seek His help and forgiveness, and we seek refuge in Allah from the evil [inclinations] of our souls and the evil [consequences] of our actions. Whoever Allah guides, none can misguide, and whomever Allah misguides, none can guide. I testify that none is worthy of worship except Allah, alone without any partner, and I testify that Muhammad was His servant and Messenger.

I – Diagnosing the Disease

Allah, the Most High, said about the hypocrites,

$$فِي قُلُوبِهِم مَّرَضٌ فَزَادَهُمُ اللَّهُ مَرَضًا$$

In their hearts is a disease, so Allah increased their disease.[1] [al-Baqara (2): 10]

$$لِيَجْعَلَ مَا يُلْقِي الشَّيْطَانُ فِتْنَةً لِّلَّذِينَ فِي قُلُوبِهِم مَّرَضٌ وَالْقَاسِيَةِ قُلُوبُهُمْ$$

---

[1] The majority of *tafsir* scholars said that the intended **"disease"** in this verse is the disease of doubts and confusions that divert from the truth. Both Ibn 'Abbâs and Ibn Mas'ood said the word **"disease"** in this verse means doubt. Even when this disease overwhelms the heart to the degree that it does away with its life altogether, it is still called a disease. The beginning of these verses testify to this fact; the Most High said, **"And of the people are some who say, 'We believe in Allah and the Last Day,' but they are not believers. They [think to] deceive Allah and those who believe, but they deceive not except themselves and perceive [it] not. In their hearts is a disease…"** [al-Baqara (2): 8-10] This is one of two types of the diseases of the heart.

The two types of the diseases of the hearts are that of *shubuhât* (doubts), and that of *shahawât* (desires). As for the disease of *shubuhât*, this refers to a corruption in perception and beliefs; a deficiency in the heart's knowledge. As for the disease of *shahawât*, this refers to a corruption in will-power, a deficiency in the heart's strength to act. The Most High said, **"…lest he whose heart is diseased become hopeful"** [al-Ahzâb (33): 32]. Whoever reflects on the diseases of the hearts that are mentioned in the Qur'an, they will find that they all fall under these two types of diseases.

[That is] so He (Allah) may make what Satan throws in a trial for those within whose hearts is disease and those hard of heart.[1] [al-Ḥajj (22): 53]

---

[1] Ibn Katheer said, "Allah destined, with His knowledge and wisdom, that Satan cast into the hearing of some people that which He never revealed anything about. The beginning of this verse attests to that; the Most High said, **'And We did not send before you any Messenger or Prophet except that when he spoke, Satan threw into his speech [some misunderstanding.'** [al-Ḥajj (22): 52] In other words, Satan casts into the hearing of some of those listening to him that which the Messenger did not actually say. Satan was only able to assault their hearts and hearing due to them being people who follow doubts and desires. The hearts of the polytheists, for instance, contained *shubuhât* such as their belief that the angels are the daughters of Allah, and that they will intercede for them before Allah, etc. Their hearts also contained the desires of pursuing prominence and leadership, and the desire to exalt their forefathers, and the likes. Due to these *shubuhât* and *shahawât* that inhabited their hearts, they received what Satan threw into their hearts and hearing as though it were the statements of the Messenger, or that it was the meaning of what the Messenger ﷺ spoke. This is not strange or far-fetched; when a person is infatuated with a particular matter, he begins to imagine that he has seen it, while in reality he has not. For example, there could be someone sitting in the dark, horrified that he will see a demon, and due to his infatuation, concern, and fear, he begins to imagine that he actually saw a demon. In the same manner, due to the polytheists' hearts being severely attached to the idols and to polytheism, they imagined that the Messenger ﷺ actually approved of their inviting to polytheism. The verse continues, **'But Allah abolishes that which Satan throws in...,'** meaning, He ﷻ annuls and removes it, **'...then, Allah makes precise His verses.'** Meaning, He ﷻ clarifies His verses completely, in a manner that unequivocally asserts *tawheed* (monotheism) and denies *shirk* (polytheism). The verses concludes, **'And Allah is Knowing and Wise,'** meaning, He ﷻ destined that based on His knowledge and wisdom. Then, the Most High explains His wisdom in destining this by saying, **'[That is] so He may make what Satan throws in a trial for those within whose hearts is a disease and those hard of heart.'** [al-Ḥajj (22): 53] In other words, it is a trial for those whose hearts contain the disease of *shubuhât*, or the disease of *shahawât*, or both. As well, it is a trial for those whose hearts are hard, whereby they do not respond or give heed, regardless of the evidences and reminders presented to them. As for the people of *eemân* (faith), they did not fall prey to what the people of *shirk*, *bid'ah* (innovation), and misguidance – whose hearts are diseased – fell into, nor did they fall into what those hard of heart fell into. The Most High said, **'And so those who were given knowledge may know that it is the truth from your Lord and [therefore] believe in it, and their hearts humbly submit to it. And indeed, Allah is the Guide of those who have believed to a straight path.'** [al-Ḥajj (22): 54]"

What Satan casts could also take place in the hearts, not in the hearing, as is the case with all the people of *bid'ah*. It is not necessary that someone hear words, which he mistakenly assumes, are the words of Allah, or the words of His Messenger ﷺ. Rather, it is possible that Satan casts into his heart incorrect meanings regarding the actual words of Allah or the actual words of His Messenger ﷺ. Satan was only capable of that due to

لَئِن لَّمْ يَنتَهِ الْمُنَافِقُونَ وَالَّذِينَ فِي قُلُوبِهِم مَّرَضٌ وَالْمُرْجِفُونَ فِي الْمَدِينَةِ لَنُغْرِيَنَّكَ بِهِمْ ثُمَّ لَا يُجَاوِرُونَكَ فِيهَا إِلَّا قَلِيلًا

---

the disease in their hearts. Otherwise, the clear proofs refute these [deviant] understandings of theirs. There is no innovator except that there exists in the Book of Allah, and the Sunnah of His Prophet ﷺ, what disproves him, just as the Qur'an used to refute all the polytheists claimed about the intercession of the angels, worshipping them, them being the daughters of Allah, and the likes.

Allah ﷻ has acquitted His Messenger ﷺ of both kinds of heart diseases by saying, **'By the star when it falls. Your companion has not erred, nor has he deviated.'** [an-Najm (53): 1-2] Acquitting [him ﷺ] of error entails that his power of knowledge was not corrupted, and acquitting [him ﷺ] of deviation entails that his power to act was not corrupted. Therefore, he ﷺ did not have any *shubuhât* or *shahawât* that would deter him from the truth.

As for the Jews and Christians, nothing destroyed them but the fact that the diseases of *shubuhât* and *shahawât* existed within their hearts. Those who incurred anger – the Jews – knew the truth but did not follow it, due to the corruption of their will-power. Those who are misguided – the Christians – did not know the truth and adopted other than it. Hence, they suffer from a corruption in their knowledge and perception, which is the basis of corrupt actions.

Both diseases – *shubuhât* and *shahawât* – plague the Jews and Christians, except that *shahawât* are more obvious in Jews, while *shubuhât* are more obvious in Christians. Also, these diseases strengthen one another, whereby the one afflicted with the disease of doubts is eventually dragged by it into the disease of desires, and the one plagued with the disease of desires is eventually dragged by it into the disease of doubts. For this reason, it is very easy for the people of sin to fall into different types of doubts, just as it is very easy for the people of innovation to fall into different types of desires. Thus, the Jews who knew the truth at first, but forsook it due to desires, were punished by later believing other than the truth. Likewise with the Christians who did not learn the truth and accepted other than it; a group of them were not inclined to desires at first, but they were later punished for not learning the truth by becoming inclined to unlawful desires and indulged in them.

As for what some reports mention about the Messenger ﷺ reciting Surat an-Najm to the polytheists, and that when he recited, **"So have you considered [the pagan idols] al-Lât and al-'Uzzâ? And Manât, the third – the other one?"** [an-Najm (53): 19-20] Satan casted upon his tongue ﷺ, "These are the supreme cranes, and their intercession is hopeful." – this is undisputedly a fabricated story, due to both its chain of transmission and its text. Hence, the casting of Satan is either in the hearts or the ears [of the listeners]; it is never in the statements of the Messenger ﷺ, but rather it is from the inspirations of Satan, may Allah's curse be upon him. [See: *Naṣb al-Majâneeq li Nasf Qissat al-Gharâneeq*, by al-Albâni, may Allah bestow his mercy upon him]

If the hypocrites, those in whose hearts is disease, and those who spread rumors in Madinah do not cease, We will surely incite you against them; then they will not remain your neighbors therein except for a little.[1] [al-Aḥzâb (33): 60]

وَلَا يَرْتَابَ الَّذِينَ أُوتُوا الْكِتَابَ وَالْمُؤْمِنُونَ وَلِيَقُولَ الَّذِينَ فِي قُلُوبِهِمْ مَرَضٌ وَالْكَافِرُونَ مَاذَا أَرَادَ اللَّهُ بِهَذَا مَثَلًا

---

[1] Many of the *tafsir* scholars said that in this context, **"those in whose hearts is disease"** is referring to the fornicators whose hearts contain the disease of desires. They used to harass women at night in the streets of Madinah, seeking to commit immorality [with them], so Allah ﷻ commanded the believing women to avoid uncovering their faces in order to distinguish themselves from the slave-girls. This would protect them from the harassment of these menaces who pursue the slave-girls because they know that corruption is more prominent among the slaves than the free women. Later, Allah ﷻ warned the hypocrites, flagrant sinners, and rumor-spreaders that if they don't desist from the mischief they were upon, He ﷻ would send against them His Messenger to expel them from Madinah.

The rumor-spreaders are those who used to evoke fear between the believers by saying: "War is upon us! The enemies have come!" – in the sense of doubting the victory [of Allah] against the likes of the Persians and Romans. They had combined between both diseases – doubts and desires. They were protective of this world, and of their lives, food, drink, security, and the likes, which generated within them a doubt in the victory of Allah ﷻ, and a belief that Islam would deteriorate, and that the enemies would annihilate the Muslims altogether. All these are manifestations of the disease of doubts; the point being that the two types of heart diseases are always paired together.

The Most High informed that these [three] types of people are **"cursed"** [al-Aḥzâb (33): 61] – meaning, expelled from the mercy of Allah. **"Wherever they are found, they are seized and massacred completely."** [al-Aḥzâb (33): 61] As-Suddi and others said, "If a man rapes a woman, his prescribed punishment is not flogging. Rather, his prescribed punishment is execution, based on the statement of the Most High regarding the fornicators and flagrant sinners who harass the believing women, **'Wherever they are found, they are seized and massacred completely.'"** This is a very strong proof regarding the matter, for rape is more of an offense to the believers than the violation of their wealth or lives.

As for the verse that confirms the existence of the disease of desires in the heart, it is the statement of the Most High, **"Then do not be soft in speech [to men] lest he whose heart is diseased become hopeful, but speak with appropriate speech."** [al-Aḥzâb (33): 32]

[So] those who were given the Scripture and the believers will not doubt and that those in whose hearts is disease and the disbelievers will say: "What does Allah intend by this as an example?"[1] [al-Muddathir (74): 31]

Also, the Most High, also said,

$$\text{يَا أَيُّهَا النَّاسُ قَدْ جَاءَتْكُمْ مَوْعِظَةٌ مِنْ رَبِّكُمْ وَشِفَاءٌ لِمَا فِي الصُّدُورِ وَهُدًى وَرَحْمَةٌ لِلْمُؤْمِنِينَ}$$

O mankind! There has come to you instruction from your Lord and healing for what is in the chests and guidance and mercy for the believers.[2] [Yoonus (10): 57]

---

[1] When Allah ﷻ strikes an example about the unseen matters, such as the number of angels appointed to the Hellfire, as the Most High said, **"Upon it are nineteen [angels]."** – the doubters whose hearts contain the disease of doubt, and the disbelievers, say, "What did Allah intend by this example?! Why did He strike for us this example?! Why did He mention to us the number of the angels?!" In fact, the disbelievers even mocked this number, and one of them – namely, Abu al-Ashdeen – who was a strong and fierce wrestler said, "O Quraysh! Handle two of them for me, and I will handle seventeen of them for you."

The Most High said, **"And We have not made their number except as a trial for those who disbelieve – so those who were given the Scripture will be convinced...,"** [al-Muddathir (74): 31] because this number is mentioned in their books as well, **"...and so those who have believed would increase in faith...,"** because every time a verse is revealed and they believe in it, this increases their faith, **"...and so those who were given the Scripture and the believers will not doubt,"** that this Qur'an which was revealed to the Messenger ﷺ is indeed the truth from Allah ﷻ. **"...And so those [hypocrites] in whose hearts is disease,"** meaning the disease of doubt, **"...and the disbelievers, will say, 'What does Allah intend by this as an example? Thus does Allah leave astray whom He wills and guides whom He wills. And none knows the soldiers of your Lord except Him."** Hence, the nineteen mentioned in this verse are only the chief angels, while the soldiers of Allah, the Blessed and High, are abundant and none knows them [all] but He ﷻ, as the Prophet ﷺ said, **"Jahannam (HellFire) will be brought on the Day of Resurrection having seventy thousand reins, and on every rein will be seventy thousand angels dragging it [forward]."** [Collected by Muslim (2842) and at-Tirmidhi (2573)]

[2] Hence, the Qur'an is a cure and an exhortation. In other words, it is a nourishment for the hearts, and a source of guidance and mercy for whoever believes in it and follows it.

وَنُنَزِّلُ مِنَ الْقُرْآنِ مَا هُوَ شِفَاءٌ وَرَحْمَةٌ لِلْمُؤْمِنِينَ وَلَا يَزِيدُ الظَّالِمِينَ إِلَّا خَسَارًا

And We send down of the Qur'an that which is healing and mercy for the believers,

but it does not increase the wrongdoers except in loss. [al-Isrâ' (17): 82]

وَيَشْفِ صُدُورَ قَوْمٍ مُؤْمِنِينَ وَيُذْهِبْ غَيْظَ قُلُوبِهِمْ

…and heal the chests of a believing people. And remove their hearts' fury.[1] [at-Tawbah

(9): 14-15]

Bodily disease is the antithesis of its health and wellbeing. It refers to a deficiency within the body – namely, that which spoils its ordinary perception and movement. Its perception may disappear [altogether] like with blindness and deafness, or it may perceive things contrary to their reality – like perceiving that which is sweet to be sour, or hallucinating things that have no reality in the tangible world.

As for its ordinary movement being spoiled, an example is losing its strength to digest [food], or detesting the nutrition that it needs, or loving the things that harm it – and it experiences pain in proportion to these [deficiencies]. Despite that, it still has not died. Rather, it retains a degree of strength by which to perform some voluntary movements, and that [disease] generates physical pain as a result of a defect in either quantity or quality.

The first is caused by either a deficiency of substance wherein it would need nutrition, or by its excess wherein it would need detoxification. The second is like intensely hot or cold temperatures, and this would [require] treatment[2].

---

[1] By the Muslims being victorious over their enemies, the Muslims' hearts are healed from the grief, trauma, and fury that plagued them due to the disbelievers subjugating them. The point being is that the heart experiences different types of diseases, and different types of cures. However, it should be noted that likes of this diseases is not dispraised in and of itself, it is like any unexpected catastrophe that a person faces and must endure patiently.

[2] In reality, bodily disease is when a part of the living body dies or stops performing its ordinary function, and consequently a person feels bodily pain and/or a loss of strength.

Likewise with the disease of the heart; it is deficiency that afflicts it and spoils its perception and will-power. [As for] its perception, this is by the *shubuhât* (doubts) that are presented to it until it cannot see the truth, or it sees it contrary to its reality. [As for] its will-power, this is by it hating the beneficial truth and by loving the harmful falsehood. For this reason, disease was at times interpreted to mean doubt and confusion, as Mujâhid and Qatâda interpreted His words, "**In their hearts is a disease**" [al-Baqara (2): 10] to mean: doubt – while other times it was interpreted as the *shahwa* (desire) of fornication, as was interpreted about His words, "**lest he whose heart is diseased become hopeful.**" [al-Ahzâb (33): 32] For this reason as well, al-Kharâ'iṭi composed his book *I'tilâl al-Quloob* – meaning the hearts' ailment – and intended by that the disease of *shahwa*.

The diseased person is bothered by that which does not bother the healthy. Thus, he is harmed by slight heat or cold, by physical exertion, or the likes of these matters, which he cannot endure due to the disease weakening him. Generally, diseases weaken those afflicted and render their strength incapable of enduring what the strong can endure.

Also, good health is preserved by its likes and removed by its opposite, and disease is strengthened by the likes of its cause and is removed by its opposite. Therefore, if the diseased incurs the likes of what caused his disease, then his diseases intensifies and his weakness increases until perhaps he dies. If he incurs what increases his strength and removes the disease, the opposite takes place.

Similarly, the disease of the heart is a pain that occurs to the heart, like being furious from an enemy that vanquished you, for that pains the heart. Allah, the Most High, said, "**…and heal the chests of a believing people. And remove the fury of their hearts.**" [at-Tawbah (9): 14-15]. Here, their healing was by removing the suffering which their hearts experienced, and [thus] it is said, 'The fury of so and so was healed,' and, 'In retaliation, there is a healing for the family of the murder victim,' and the likes. They were the remedy for the grief, fury, and sorrow, which are all pains that occur within oneself.

Therefore, just as bodily disease is a deficiency in its life, the heart's disease is also a condition where its life is deficient or has died partially.

Similarly, doubt and ignorance pain the heart. The Prophet ﷺ said, **"Should they not have asked when they did not know? Indeed, the cure for ignorance is but a question."**[1] The heart of an individual who is doubtful and hesitant regarding a matter is pained until he acquires certain knowledge. Thus, it is said about the scholar who clarifies the truth with his response, "He has healed me with [his] response."

Disease is less than death; the heart dies from absolute ignorance[2] and becomes diseased from a shade of ignorance. Hence, it can experience death and disease as well as life and health – and its life, death, disease, and cure are greater than the body's life, death, disease, and cure. For this reason, if the heart's disease is subjected to a *shubha* or *shahwa*, the disease intensifies, and when it is subjected to wisdom and exhortation, this works towards its wellbeing and cure[3].

The Most High said, **"[That is] so He (Allah) may make what Satan throws in a trial for those within whose hearts is disease,"** – because this generates a doubt in them – **"and those hard of heart,"** [al-Ḥajj (22): 53] – due to its dryness. Their hearts were weakened by the disease, so what Satan threw became a trial for them, and the hardness of their hearts distanced them from *eemân* (faith), so it became a trial for them.

Similarly, the Most High said, **"If the hypocrites, those in whose hearts is disease, and those who spread rumors in Madinah do not cease,"** [al-Aḥzâb (33): 60] – just as the Most High said, **"And that those in whose hearts is disease and the disbelievers will say…"**[4] [al-Muddathir (74): 31]. Their hearts did not die like the death of

---

[1] Narrated by Abu Dâwud in *as-Sunan* (336), and al-Albâni deemed it *ḥasan* without the statement, "It would have been sufficient for him…" in *Ṣaḥeeḥ Abu Dâwud* (335).

[2] Absolute ignorance is referring to the complete ignorance of the disbelievers whose hearts have died as a result of associating others with Allah ﷻ. As for his words, "a shade of ignorance," this is referring to a lesser degree – that of partial ignorance. Ignorance is either when the truth is not known to begin with, or by believing what is contrary to it.

[3] Its wisdom teaches him and its exhortation reminds him. Therefore, the wisdom strengthens his knowledge (power to understand), and the exhortation strengthens his resolve (power to act).

[4] In these two verses, He ﷻ paired between **"those in whose hearts is disease"** and **"the hypocrites,"** and then paired between **"the disbelievers"** and **"those in whose hearts is disease."** By doing that, it becomes clear that those in whose hearts is disease are neither disbelievers nor hypocrites. Rather, they only have a shade of disbelief and

the disbelievers and hypocrites, nor is it well and healthy like the health of the believers' hearts. Rather, it contains the diseases of *shubha* and *shahwa*.

Likewise, **"lest he whose heart is diseased become hopeful,"** [al-Aḥzâb (33): 32] – refers to the disease of *shahwa*. Were the healthy heart subjected to a woman, it would not turn towards her, whereas the heart diseased with desires would turn to this when subjected to it – because of its weakness – in proportion to the strength or weakness of the disease. For that reason, when she is soft in speech, he whose heart is diseased becomes hopeful[1].

II – The Qur'an is a Remedy

The Qur'an is a remedy for what is in the chests. Whoever's heart contains the diseases of doubts and desires, it (the Qur'an) contains the clear proofs that distinguish truth from falsehood[2]. It removes the disease of doubt, which spoils knowledge, perception, and realization – whereby he can see things as they actually are. It contains wisdom, excellent exhortation via encouraging [good] and frightening [from evil], and stories which contain lessons that promote health in the heart. As a result, the heart becomes inclined to what brings it benefit and disinclined towards what brings it harm. After desiring deviance and detesting guidance, the heart now loves guidance and detests deviance.

Therefore, the Qur'an removes the diseases which evoke corrupt desires. This purifies the heart, which in turn purifies its desire, and consequently returns it to its *fiṭra* (natural state) upon which it was disposed – just as the body returns to its normal state.

---

hypocrisy. However, the Qur'an does sometimes use the term "diseased heart" in reference to major hypocrisy – as we previously mentioned – and that is recognized by the context indicators and other corroborating evidences.

[1] Giving in to desires happens at heart first, and then the limbs follow. Therefore, when a person is not able to lower his gaze, or guard his private parts, or the likes, that is all due to the diseased state of his heart. Were his heart healthy, he would have rejected that [notion], and would have been bothered by flirtatious speech, immodest dressing, and all other kinds of sin.

[2] In other words, he would be capable of discerning truth from falsehood, especially at times when they are mixed or confused for one another.

III – Nourishing the Heart

The heart is nourished with what purifies and strengthens it through *eemân* and the Qur'an, just as the body is nourished through what strengthens and develops it – for the purification of the heart is like the development of the body[1].

Linguistically, *zakâh* means development and growing healthily. It is said, 'The matter underwent *zakâh*," when it has grown healthily. The heart requires nourishment in order to develop, and become healthy and complete[2] – just as the body requires being nourished with that which benefits it. Alongside that, that which harms it must be guarded against. Therefore, the body does not develop without being given what benefits it and safeguarded against what harms it. Likewise with the heart – it does not become purified, grow, and reach full health without acquiring what benefits it and repelling what harms it. And also with plants – they do not develop without this[3].

Since charity extinguishes the sins just as water extinguishes fire[4], the heart undergoes *zakâh* through it, and its *zakâh* is beyond [merely] being purified from sin[5]. Allah, the Most High, said,

---

[1] The heart is predisposed upon loving the Sharia (laws) of Allah ﷻ, preferring it, and hating what opposes the Sharia. Hence, were the heart still upon its *fiṭra* (original disposition), it would never have harbored these corrupt desires which are centered on loving that which harms it. The Qur'an removes these corrupt desires from the heart until it returns to the *fiṭra* upon which Allah [initially] created it.

[2] It develops and increases so that s/he can witness the realities of *eemân* and gain more of them.

[3] Just as plants require irrigation and fertilizer, and just as they require someone to remove the harmful weeds, likewise is the heart; it requires both being rectified via acts of worship, and being protected from the evil, unlawful elements that harm it. For this reason, were someone to perform some acts of obedience, while he listens to unlawful things, such as music, backbiting, and gossip, and doesn't lower his gaze, and the like – then how can his heart thrive? That is like an injured person to whom you give a dose of blood, but leave his many wounds hemorrhaging continuously."

[4] Narrated by at-Tirmidhi (2616), Aḥmad (15319), and al-Albâni deemed it authentic in *Ṣaḥeeḥ al-Jâmi'* (5136). The wording [here] is that of at-Tirmidhi, on the authority of Mu'âdh ibn Jabal ﷺ.

[5] Therefore, purifying the heart from sins is the first step to *tazkiya*, just as it is said, "*takhliya* (detoxification) must happen before *taḥliya* (beautification)."

$$\text{خُذْ مِنْ أَمْوَالِهِمْ صَدَقَةً تُطَهِّرُهُمْ وَتُزَكِّيهِمْ بِهَا}$$

Take [O Muhammad] from their wealth a charity by which you purify them and cause them *zakâh* (increase). [at-Tawbah (9): 103]

As well, abandoning immorality and sin purify the heart, for these are comparable to toxins in the body and weeds in plants. Once the body is detoxified of these foul substances – like draining excess blood – then the body can rest, retrieve its original strength, and thereby grow. Likewise, once one repents from the sins, this detoxifies his [contaminated] mixture – for he has mixed between righteous and wicked acts. So when one repents from [his] sins, the heart's strength and will-power to perform righteous acts is liberated, and the heart finds relief from the detrimental effects that were inside of it. Therefore, the *zakâh* of the heart involves its growth and completeness. The Most High said,

$$\text{وَلَوْلَا فَضْلُ اللَّهِ عَلَيْكُمْ وَرَحْمَتُهُ مَا زَكَى مِنكُم مِّنْ أَحَدٍ أَبَدًا}$$

And if not for the bounty of Allah upon you and His mercy, none of you would have *zakâ* (become pure).[1] [an-Noor (24): 21]

$$\text{وَإِن قِيلَ لَكُمُ ارْجِعُوا فَارْجِعُوا هُوَ أَزْكَى لَكُمْ}$$

And if it is said to you, 'Go back.' – then go back; it is *azkâ* (purer) for you.[1] [an-Noor (24): 28]

---

[1] This verse was revealed after the incident of *al-Ifk* (the Slander) to establish that those whom Allah ﷻ protected from gossiping about this scandal were only saved by Allah's bounty and mercy. He ﷻ is the One who purified them from indulging in backbiting, gossip, and falsely accusing people of fornication. On the other hand, the gatherings of the hypocrites – in every age – are always filled with talk of immorality. Nowadays, we find most magazines, television series', and movies focusing heavily on spreading immorality between people, making up countless stories that all serve that end. This is of the signs of hypocrisy and the heart being diseased.

قُلْ لِلْمُؤْمِنِينَ يَغُضُّوا مِنْ أَبْصَارِهِمْ وَيَحْفَظُوا فُرُوجَهُمْ ذَلِكَ أَزْكَى لَهُمْ

Tell the believing men to reduce from their gaze and guard their private parts. That is *azkâ* (purer) for them. Indeed, Allah is fully informed about what they do.[2] [an-Noor (24): 30]

قَدْ أَفْلَحَ مَنْ تَزَكَّى وَذَكَرَ اسْمَ رَبِّهِ فَصَلَّى

He has certainly succeeded who *tazakkâ* (purifies himself). And mentions the name of his Lord and prays. [al-A'lâ (87): 14-15]

قَدْ أَفْلَحَ مَنْ زَكَّاهَا وَقَدْ خَابَ مَنْ دَسَّاهَا

He has certainly succeeded who *zakkâha* (purifies it). And he has certainly failed who buries it [into corruption].[3] [ash-Shams (91): 9-10]

---

[1] In other words, just as the heart undergoes *tazkiya* via abandoning immorality, it also undergoes *tazkiya* via humbleness. Whoever is told, "Go back," and he surrenders to the ruling of Allah ﷻ and harbors no objection to that, he has thereby humbled himself for Allah. As for the arrogant, he becomes angry, for he feels that he has a lofty status, and that the door should be opened from the moment he knocks.

[2] This indicates that gazing at the unlawful blinds the heart, and lowering the gaze grants it light and vision. Just as one of the *salaf* said, "Whoever lowers his *basar* (eyesight), Allah enlightens his *baseera* (insight)." Perhaps this is the secret behind Surat an-Noor (the Light) having that name, due to what it contains of the rulings that illuminate the heart via abandoning desires, such as the prohibition of fornication, falsely accusing others of fornication, and gazing at the unlawful, as well as establishing the rulings related to seeking permission [before entering private places], *hijâb* (veiling), and the likes.

[3] In other words, successful is the one whom Allah purifies and nourishes with *taqwâ*, just as he ﷺ said, **"Allâhumma Âti Nafsee Taqwâhâ, Zakkihâ Anta Khayru Man Zakkâhâ, Anta Waliyyuhâ wa Mawlâhâ (O Allah, grant my inner-self its taqwâ (piety); purify it (my inner-self), for You are the best to purify it; You are its Guardian and its Master)."** [Collected by Muslim (2722), an-Nasâ'i (5458), Ahmad (19327), and al-Albâni authenticated it in *Saheeh al-Jâmi'* (1286)]

Due to Shaykh al-Islâm's citation of this verse here, it appears that he intended the alternate meaning which some *tafsir* scholars gave regarding it. The first view we mentioned is that the doer in **"zakkâhâ (he who purifies it)"** is Allah ﷻ, and this view

$$\text{وَمَا يُدْرِيكَ لَعَلَّهُ يَزَّكَّى}$$

But what would make you perceive [O Muhammad] that perhaps he may *yazzakkâ* (become purified).[1] ['Abasa (80): 3]

$$\text{فَقُلْ هَلْ لَكَ إِلَى أَنْ تَزَكَّى وَأَهْدِيَكَ إِلَى رَبِّكَ فَتَخْشَى}$$

And say [to Fir'awn], 'Would you [be willing to] *tazakkâ* (purify yourself)? And let me guide you to your Lord so you would fear [Him]?' [an-Nâzi'ât (79): 18-19]

Even though the basis of *tazkiya* is growth, blessing, and an increase in goodness, it can only be attained by removing the evil. For this reason, *tazkiya* was inclusive of both this and that, and thus He ﷻ said,

$$\text{وَوَيْلٌ لِلْمُشْرِكِينَ الَّذِينَ لَا يُؤْتُونَ الزَّكَاةَ}$$

Woe to those who associate [others with Allah] – those who do not fulfill *zakâh*.[2]

[Fuṣṣilat (41): 6-7]

---

is supported by the [incident when the] Messenger of Allah ﷺ recited it in relation to *qadar* (fate). The second view is that the doer in **"zakkâhâ (he who purifies it)"** is the slave; the slave seeks to purify himself, and as a result is successful. This view is supported by the words of the Most High, **"He has certainly succeeded who tazakkâ (purifies himself)."** [al-A'lâ (87): 14] However, the first view is stronger regarding the meaning of this verse due to the mentioned hadith. Nonetheless, the second view is still correct in and of itself, as a fact.

[1] This was revealed about 'Abdullâh b. Umm Maktoom ؓ, when he came to the Prophet ﷺ asking him about Islam. Therefore, the *zakâh* (purification) here is caused by the knowledge which generates the fear of Allah ﷻ.

[2] The majority of *tafsir* scholars from among the *salaf* view that the meaning of *zakâh* in this verse is *tawḥeed* (monotheism) and *eemân* (faith). Hence, this is the basis for the *tazkiya* of any soul.

Zakâh here refers to the *tawheed* (monotheism) and *eemân* which nourish the heart, for they involve denying the divinity of anyone but *al-Haqq* (Allah) from the heart, and [then] by affirming the divinity of *al-Haqq* in that heart. This is the reality of *Lâ Elâha Illâ Allâh*, which is the basis upon which the hearts become nourished.

Tazkiya is the act of deeming something pure, whether intrinsically or in belief and perception, just as one says, "*'Addaltuh* (I deemed him credible)." – when he deemed him credible in actuality, or in the perception of the people. The Most High said:

$$فَلَا تُزَكُّوا أَنفُسَكُمْ هُوَ أَعْلَمُ بِمَنِ اتَّقَى$$

So do not *tuzakku* (deem pure) yourselves. He knows best of who fears Him. [an-Najm (53): 32]

This means: do not claim its purity[1]. This is other than His statement, **"He has certainly succeeded who *zakkâha* (purifies it),"**[2] [ash-Shams (91): 9] and that is why He said [in the former], **"He is most knowing of who fears Him."** [an-Najm (53): 32]

---

[1] In other words, this verse does not mean the slave shouldn't strive to purify himself. Rather, it means that he should not praise himself and say that his inner-self is pure.

[2] Meaning, he has certainly succeeded who purifies and refines himself. It would have been more correct here to mention the words of the Most High, **"He has certainly succeeded who *tazakkâ* (purifies himself)."** [al-A'lâ (87): 14] This is because they differed on the meaning of **"*zakkâha* (he who purifies it),"** whether the pronoun was referring to Allah or the slave. Therefore, the verse either means he has succeeded who purifies and refines himself, or he has succeeded who has been purified by Allah. The two interpretations are factually correct, although it is more correct to mention the other verse here which clearly refers to the slave purifying himself. As for how the two interpretations are related, that is because Allah ﷻ does not purify a slave unless the slave works for that and strives to purify himself, as the Most High said, **"And those who pursue guidance – He increases them in guidance and grants them their taqwâ (piety)."** [Muhammad (47): 17] At the same time, purifying oneself is not possible without seeking protection with Allah ﷻ and relying on Him, just as the Messenger ﷺ used to say, **"*Allâhumma Âti Nafsee Taqwâhâ, Zakkihâ Anta Khayru Man Zakkâhâ* (O Allah, grant my inner-self its *taqwâ* (piety); purify it (my inner-self), for You are the best to purify it)."** Hence, the one who strives to purify himself without relying on Allah or seeking His help, but rather relies on himself and is confident in his strength, will be striving for nothing and will never attain purity.

The name of Zaynab ﷺ used to be Barra (Pure One), and it was said that she was claimingity to herself, so the Messenger of Allah ﷺ named her Zaynab[1].

As for His statement,

$$
\text{أَلَمْ تَرَ إِلَى الَّذِينَ يُزَكُّونَ أَنْفُسَهُمْ بَلِ اللَّهُ يُزَكِّي مَنْ يَشَاءُ}
$$

Have you not seen those who *yuzakkoon* (deem purity) of themselves? Rather, Allah purifies whom He wills... [an-Nisâ' (4): 49]

This means they consider it pure and inform of its purity[2], just as someone who qualifies a witness and informs of him being *'adl* (credible).

IV – Between Justice and Oppression

'Adl (justice) entails uprightness, and uprightness entails the soundness of the heart – just as *dhulm* (oppression) entails its corruption. For this reason, every sin involves a man being a *dhâlim* (oppressor) to himself[3]. The opposite of *dhulm* is *'adl*, and hence [the sinner] has not been *'adl* with himself, rather he has oppressed it.

Therefore, the soundness of heart lies in *'adl* and its corruption lies in *dhulm*. Also, when the slave oppresses himself, he is the oppressor and the oppressed. Likewise, when he is just and upright, then he is the performer and recipient of that justice. This is because the

---

[1] Collected by al-Bukhâri (5839), Muslim (2141), and Ibn Mâjah (3732).

[2] So, He ﷺ criticized those who informed about themselves that they were righteous, and informed that He ﷺ is the One who knows matters as they truly are, just as He ﷺ is the One who possesses the ability to purify the hearts and souls.

[3] *Dhulm* (injustice) is placing a thing in other than its rightful place. So when the slave doesn't rectify his heart and corrupts it instead, he has oppressed himself by placing it in other than the state He was commanded to. For this reason, the sinner oppresses himself in this world before the Hereafter, due to the stress, grief, difficulties, and other immediate punishments that befall him. The greatest sin is *shirk* (associating others) with Allah ﷺ , due to it being the greatest *dhulm*, and we seek Allah's refuge from that.

action originates from him, and upon him returns the fruit of that action, whether it is good or evil. The Most High said,

$$لَهَا مَا كَسَبَتْ وَعَلَيْهَا مَا اكْتَسَبَتْ$$

It will have what [good] it has gained, and it will bear what [evil] it has earned. [al-Baqara (2): 286]

Actions affect the heart – whether it benefits or harms – before affecting the external body, and hence their soundness is justice to it and their corruption is an oppression of it[1]. The Most High said,

$$مَنْ عَمِلَ صَالِحًا فَلِنَفْسِهِ وَمَنْ أَسَاءَ فَعَلَيْهَا$$

Whoever does righteousness – it is for his [own] soul; and whoever does evil – it is against it. [Fuṣṣilat (41): 46]

$$إِنْ أَحْسَنْتُمْ أَحْسَنْتُمْ لِأَنْفُسِكُمْ وَإِنْ أَسَأْتُمْ فَلَهَا$$

If you do good, you do good for yourselves; and if you do evil, then it is to them (yourselves). [al-Isrâ' (17): 7]

---

[1] From the moment a person decides to commit an act of obedience or a sin, there occurs in his heart a form of health or corruption, in proportion to what he was determined to commit. Then, when he actually performs the sin, its external effects surface. Therefore, the earthquakes, disasters, diseases, famines, droughts, and every other type of corruption are but the effects of sins. The Most High said, **"Corruption has appeared throughout the land and sea by [reason of] what the hands of people have earned, so He may let them taste part of [the consequence of] what they have done, so that perhaps they will return [to righteousness]."** [ar-Room (30): 41] The worst of these effects is that which happens to the heart of a person once he decides to commit a sin or *shirk*, and we seek Allah's refuge from that.

One of the *salaf* (predecessors) said, "A good deed generates light in the heart[1], strength in the body[2], brightness in the face, expanse in sustenance, and love in the hearts of the creation. An evil deed causes darkness in the heart, blackness in the face, weakness in the body, decrease in sustenance, and hatred in the hearts of the creation."

The Most High said,

$$كُلُّ امْرِئٍ بِمَا كَسَبَ رَهِينٌ$$

Every person, by what he has earned, is kept hostage. [aṭ-Ṭoor (52): 21]

$$كُلُّ نَفْسٍ بِمَا كَسَبَتْ رَهِينَةٌ$$

Every soul, for what it has earned, will be kept hostage. [al-Muddathir (74): 38]

$$وَذَكِّرْ بِهِ أَنْ تُبْسَلَ نَفْسٌ بِمَا كَسَبَتْ لَيْسَ لَهَا مِنْ دُونِ اللَّهِ وَلِيٌّ وَلَا شَفِيعٌ وَإِنْ تَعْدِلْ كُلَّ عَدْلٍ لَا يُؤْخَذْ مِنْهَا أُولَئِكَ الَّذِينَ أُبْسِلُوا بِمَا كَسَبُوا$$

But remind with it (the Qur'an), lest a soul be taken captive due to what it earned; it will have other than Allah no protector and no intercessor. And if it should offer every

---

[1] A light by which he can see matters as they [really] are. Hence, sees the truth as truth and falsehood as falsehood. It also enables him to gauge things properly, assessing their value just as it is in the sight of Allah; he aggrandizes that which is [actually] grand, and despises that which is [actually] despicable. Furthermore, this light causes him not to rush fate, nor to be deceived by false hopes.

[2] One of the *salaf*, who was eighty years old, once jumped a distance that a young man could not. Those around him were amazed by this, so he said to them, "We safeguarded this body for Allah when we were young, so Allah safeguarded it for us when we became old." Similarly, the Prophet ﷺ began his battlefield jihad at the age of 53, and Abu Bakr ؓ was also 53 years old at that time. All this is from the blessings of living in obedience to Allah ﷻ .

'**adl** (ransom)[1], it would not be taken from it. Those are the ones who are taken captive due to what they have earned.** [al-An'âm (6): 70]

Tubsal [in this verse] means to be taken hostage, to be imprisoned, or to be captured.

Furthermore, when the body returns to health from a disease, it is said: "His temperament has become upright." – because disease is but the displacement of temperament – even though complete uprightness which is void of blemish cannot be attained. Yet, what is most ideal should still be sought.

The likes of this applies to the heart; its health lies in *'adl* and its disease lies in deviance and *dhulm*. Surely, absolute *'adl* in all matters is impossible, and this is known factually and through experience, but what is *amthal* (most ideal) should still be sought. This is what is intended by one saying, "This is *amthal*," and is the intent behind saying that the *salafī* methodology is the path, which is *muthlâ*. The Most High said,

$$وَلَنْ تَسْتَطِيعُوا أَنْ تَعْدِلُوا بَيْنَ النِّسَاءِ وَلَوْ حَرَصْتُمْ$$

And you will never be able to be equal [in feeling] between wives, even if you should strive [to do so]. [an-Nisâ' (4): 129]

$$وَأَوْفُوا الْكَيْلَ وَالْمِيزَانَ بِالْقِسْطِ لَا نُكَلِّفُ نَفْسًا إِلَّا وُسْعَهَا$$

And give full measure and weight in justice. We do not charge any soul except [with that within] its capacity. [al-An'âm (6): 152]

Allah, the Most High, sent the messengers and revealed the books so that the people may uphold justice, and the greatest justice is worshipping Allah alone without any

---

[1] Linguistically, *al-'adl* refers to that which is equal. Thus, **"and if it should offer every 'adl…"** means that if it should bring every form of equivalent, as a ransom in exchange for its rescue, even if it were the Earth's fill of gold, none of that would be accepted.

partner, and then upholding *'adl* regarding the rights of humanity, and then upholding *'adl* with yourself. *Dhulm* is also three types[1], and every *dhulm* is from the diseases of the hearts, and [every] *'adl* entails its soundness and health.

Aḥmad b. Ḥanbal said to an individual, "If you were healthy, you would not have feared anyone." In other words, your fear of the creation is from a disease within you, such as the disease of *shirk* and sin.

V – The Heart's Life & Illumination

Essentially, the soundness of the heart is its life and its illumination. The Most High said,

$$أَوَمَن كَانَ مَيْتًا فَأَحْيَيْنَاهُ وَجَعَلْنَا لَهُ نُورًا يَمْشِي بِهِ فِي النَّاسِ كَمَن مَّثَلُهُ فِي الظُّلُمَاتِ لَيْسَ بِخَارِجٍ مِّنْهَا$$

And is one who was dead and We gave him life and made for him light by which to walk among the people like one who is in darkness, never to emerge therefrom?[2] [al-An'âm (6): 122]

---

[1] *Dhulm* is three types; there is the slave committing *dhulm* to others, there is his *dhulm* of himself (with sins lesser than major *shirk*), and there is major *dhulm* which is committing *shirk* (associating others) with Allah.

[2] This is the example of a believer who believes after being upon disbelief and misguidance, and that of a disbeliever whom Allah knows will not believe. The example of the believer who believes after being upon disbelief is that he was **"dead,"** meaning during his disbelief, **"and We gave him life,"** meaning through *eemân*, **"and made for him light,"** meaning a light by which he discerns truth from falsehood, and guidance from misguidance, **"by which to walk among the people,"** meaning he sees his way between the peoples' difference. **"[Is] he like one who is in darkness, never to emerge therefrom?"** This is the example of the disbeliever whom Allah knows will not believe. The point of reference in this verse is that Allah ﷻ described the believer with the qualities of life and light, and this is the meaning of Shaykh al-Islâm Ibn Taymiya's words, "Essentially, the soundness of the heart is its life and its illumination."

For this reason, Allah mentions the life of the hearts and their brightness, and their death and their darkness, in several places. For instance, He ﷺ said,

$$لِيُنذِرَ مَن كَانَ حَيًّا وَيَحِقَّ الْقَوْلُ عَلَى الْكَافِرِينَ$$

To warn whoever is alive and justify the word (decree) against the disbelievers.[1]

[YâSeen (36): 70]

$$يَا أَيُّهَا الَّذِينَ آمَنُوا اسْتَجِيبُوا لِلَّهِ وَلِلرَّسُولِ إِذَا دَعَاكُمْ لِمَا يُحْيِيكُمْ وَاعْلَمُوا أَنَّ اللَّهَ يَحُولُ بَيْنَ الْمَرْءِ وَقَلْبِهِ وَأَنَّهُ إِلَيْهِ تُحْشَرُونَ$$

O you who have believed, respond to Allah and to the Messenger when he calls you to that which gives you life, and know that Allah intervenes between a man and his heart, and that to Him you shall all be gathered.[2] [al-Anfâl (8): 24]

---

[1] In other words, only the believer benefits from the warning. As for the disbelievers, it justifies their predestined fate that Allah ﷺ had written regarding them, namely them deserving – in all fairness – His punishment of them. The point of reference is that Allah ﷺ described the believers here with the quality of life.

[2] The statement of Allah ﷺ, **"respond to Allah and to the Messenger when he calls you to that which gives you life,"** means when he calls you to the various acts of obedience through which the hearts come to life. Hence, the living heart is that which recognizes truth from falsehood, seeks the face of Allah, the Blessed and High, and strives to earn His pleasure. In turn, he finds a delight, and the sweetness of *eemân*, in his heart. Then, He said, **"and know that Allah intervenes between a man and his heart,"** meaning He intervenes between a disbeliever and *eemân*, and between a sinner and obedience, just as He intervenes between a believer and disbelief, and between an obedient slave and sin. As for the disbeliever and sinner, when Allah ﷺ invited them to life the first time and they refused, were arrogant, and neglected – He ﷺ intervened between them and *eemân* and obedience. Thus, you find them recognizing the truth but incapable of following it because Allah severed between them and their hearts. Likewise with the believer and the obedient, when they responded to Allah and to the Messenger ﷺ, their hearts became alive from that. Thus, the moment sins and desires are presented to such a living heart, they are immediately rejected due to the strength of its life. This is all a repayment from Allah, the Blessed and High, to these people for their obeying Him, and their responding to Allah and His Messenger ﷺ. Hence, actions inevitably affect the heart.

Similarly, He ﷻ said,

$$ يُخْرِجُ الْحَيَّ مِنَ الْمَيِّتِ وَيُخْرِجُ الْمَيِّتَ مِنَ الْحَيِّ $$

He brings the living out of the dead and brings the dead out of the living. [ar-Room (30): 19]

… and of its types is bringing forth a believer from a disbeliever, and bringing forth a disbeliever from a believer[1].

In the authentic hadith as well, **"The similitude of a house that remembers Allah and a house that does not remember Allah is like that of the living and the dead."[2]** Also, in *as-Saheeh*, **"Allot your homes [a share] from your prayers, and do not deem them graveyards."[34]**

Allah, the Most High, also said,

$$ وَالَّذِينَ كَذَّبُوا بِآيَاتِنَا صُمٌّ وَبُكْمٌ فِي الظُّلُمَاتِ $$

---

[1] Many of the *salaf* gave this interpretation to such verses, citing how Allah brought Ibrâheem ﷺ out from his father, Âzar, and brought out of Nooh ﷺ his disbelieving son. Although this verse supports that meaning, it is actually more general than just that. It also includes Him ﷻ bringing out the living chick from an egg that doesn't appear to be alive, and Him ﷻ bringing out plants from water and dust, and Him ﷻ bringing out lifeless objects from the living bodies of the human and animal, and the likes.

[2] Collected by Muslim (779) and Ibn Hibbân (854). It was also collected by al-Bukhâri (6407) with similar wording.

[3] Collected by Muslim (777), Ahmad in *al-Musnad* (24411, 4653), and al-Bayhaqi in *as-Sunan al-Kubrâ* (2860).

[4] In other words, Allah ﷻ gives life to the people of a household because of the prayers that are established in it. As for the house wherein no prayer is established, it is dead like the graveyard which is not prayed in.

But those who deny Our verses are deaf and dumb within darknesses.[1] [al-An'âm (6): 39]

Allah, the Glorified, mentioned the "Verse of Light" and "Verse of Darkness" wherein He said,

اللَّهُ نُورُ السَّمَاوَاتِ وَالْأَرْضِ مَثَلُ نُورِهِ كَمِشْكَاةٍ فِيهَا مِصْبَاحٌ الْمِصْبَاحُ فِي زُجَاجَةٍ الزُّجَاجَةُ كَأَنَّهَا كَوْكَبٌ دُرِّيٌّ يُوقَدُ مِن شَجَرَةٍ مُّبَارَكَةٍ زَيْتُونَةٍ لَّا شَرْقِيَّةٍ وَلَا غَرْبِيَّةٍ يَكَادُ زَيْتُهَا يُضِيءُ وَلَوْ لَمْ تَمْسَسْهُ نَارٌ نُّورٌ عَلَى نُورٍ

Allah is the Light of the heavens and the earth. The example of His light is like a niche within which is a lantern, the lamp is within glass, the glass as if it were a pearly [white] star lit from [the oil of] a blessed olive tree, neither of the east nor the west, whose oil would almost glow even if untouched by fire. Light upon light.[2] [an-Noor (24): 35]

---

[1] They do not see the truth nor hear it, for they are in the darknesses of ignorance, and we seek Allah's refuge from that.

[2] Regarding the words of the Most High, **"Allah is the Light of the heavens and the earth,"** Ibn Mas'ood said, "The light of the heavens and the earth is from the light of His face." He ﷻ is described with every trait of perfection and praise, and since light is a praiseworthy quality in His creation, then He ﷻ is more deserving of such perfection – but in a manner befitting Him ﷻ. Hence, Allah is an-Noor al-Hâdi (the Light, the Guide). As for the words of Ibn Mas'ood ﷺ, they mean that the light of the heavens and earth is one of the effects of His quality of light. In other words, He would not have created light, had it not been one of His qualities to begin with. Therefore, every praiseworthy quality in the creation is an effect of the perfect qualities of the Creator ﷻ. Describing Him, the Mighty and Majestic, with the quality of light cannot mean that it is like the light of the creation. Rather, it is just like us saying that the mercy in the hearts of the slaves is from the mercy of Allah, the Blessed and High, meaning one of the effects of His mercy. Neither the light of the creation, nor the mercy that has been created, are a part of His qualities. Exalted is Allah above existing in anything of His creation.

Then, He ﷻ gave an example for the light of *eemân* in the heart of His believing slave, and said, **"The example of His light,"** meaning in the heart of His believing slave, **"is like a niche,"** and a niche is that indent in the wall where lamps are placed. **"In it is a lantern,"** meaning inside this niche is a lantern, and a lantern is a lamp whose wick burns to generate light. **"The lantern is within glass,"** because the lantern that isn't protected by glass is subject to the wind, whereas the light of a lantern encased in glass is stable and consistent. **"The glass – as if it were a pearly [white] star,"** meaning the light of this lantern which glows from within the glass resembles the light of a bright star. **"Lit from a blessed tree,"** meaning this lantern is fueled by the oil of a tree of abundant goodness. **"An olive tree - neither of the east nor the west,"** meaning it is fueled by the oil of an olive tree. This tree is neither eastern, whereby the sun would only strike it in the early daylight hours, nor western, whereby the sun would only strike in the late daylight hours, because trees are frequently found in the shade of a mountain, or the likes. Instead, this tree is struck by the sun throughout the day, and the best olive oil comes from the likes of these trees which are situated upon a mountaintop or in the middle of a wide plateau. This is the meaning of, **"neither of the east nor the west."** It is not just eastern or western, rather it is both eastern and western, whereby the sun strikes it as it rises and as it sets. And this oil, from the intensity of its purity and shine, **"would almost glow even if untouched by fire."** Then, when the fire actually touches it, it generates the most perfect light, making it **"light upon light."**

The niche is the chest of the believing slave, and the glass is his heart. The illuminating lantern is the revelation that descends [from Allah], and the pure olive oil is the sound *fiṭra*. The believer could almost recognize the truth with the light of his *fiṭra*, so when the revelation comes and coincides with the sound *fiṭra*, it becomes light upon light. The believer's heart was resembled with glass here because glass combines between the qualities of solidity and transparency. The transparency indicates that light enters into it and exits from it as well. Hence, the believer has *eemân* enter his heart, and he illuminates with the light of his *eemân* the hearts of those around him. He illuminates for them the path to Allah, just as the Companions of the Messenger ﷺ used to illuminate the path for humanity, and consequently they would become guided via their guidance. This was only made possible by the light they themselves had acquired from the guiding light, Muhammad ﷺ. Likewise was the case with all the Prophets; they used to guide the people by virtue of the light in their hearts. As for solidity, this indicates being steadfast upon the truth, unlike liquids which undertake the form of whatever container they are poured into. Hence, the believer's heart is constant upon the truth. It does not change or overturn with the changing events and circumstances, as oppose to the heart of the hypocrite. Similarly, the Prophet ﷺ likened the believer's heart, with regards to how it reacts to *fitna* (tribulation), to that of a white stone. He ﷺ said, **"The *fitan* (trials) are presented to the hearts like a straw mat, one straw after another. Whichever heart absorbs them has a black spot stamped onto it, and whichever heart rejects them has a white spot stamped onto it. This continues until the hearts become [one of] two types: a heart which is white and smooth, like a polished stone, that will not be harmed by the *fitan* for as long as the heavens and earth remain, and another heart which is black and blemished, like an overturned jug, that neither acknowledges the right nor rejects the wrong, except for that which happens to coincide with its desires which it absorbed."**

وَالَّذِينَ كَفَرُوا أَعْمَالُهُمْ كَسَرَابٍ بِقِيعَةٍ يَحْسَبُهُ الظَّمْآنُ مَاءً حَتَّى إِذَا جَاءَهُ لَمْ يَجِدْهُ شَيْئًا وَوَجَدَ اللَّهَ عِنْدَهُ فَوَفَّاهُ حِسَابَهُ وَاللَّهُ سَرِيعُ الْحِسَابِ ۝ أَوْ كَظُلُمَاتٍ فِي بَحْرٍ لُجِّيٍّ يَغْشَاهُ مَوْجٌ مِنْ فَوْقِهِ مَوْجٌ مِنْ فَوْقِهِ سَحَابٌ ظُلُمَاتٌ بَعْضُهَا فَوْقَ بَعْضٍ إِذَا أَخْرَجَ يَدَهُ لَمْ يَكَدْ يَرَاهَا وَمَنْ لَمْ يَجْعَلِ اللَّهُ لَهُ نُورًا فَمَا لَهُ مِنْ نُورٍ

But those who disbelieved – their deeds are like a mirage in a lowland which a thirsty one thinks is water until, when he comes to it, he finds it is nothing but finds Allah before him, and He will pay him in full his due; and Allah is swift in account. Or [they are] like darknesses within an unfathomable sea, which is covered by waves, upon which are waves, over which are clouds – darknesses, some of them upon others. When one pulls out his hand [therein], he can hardly see it. And he to whom Allah has not granted light – for him there is no light.[1] [an-Noor (24): 39-40]

[Narrated by Muslim (144) and Ahmad (23487 & 23328)] Whiteness symbolizes clear insight, and solidity symbolizes steadfastness on the truth, and this is the epitome of a heart's knowledge and will-power.

[1] In these verses are two examples of the disbelievers. The first verse is an example of the leaders of misguidance who believe in falsehood and assume it to be truth. They are like the thirsty person who sees a mirage and assumes it to be water. Likewise, they assume that their actions will benefit them with Allah, but when they come on the Day of Recompense, it will be as if these actions never existed. Instead, they will find Allah before them – to recompense them for their disbelief – and Allah is swift in account.

The second verse is an example of the masses of disbelievers who imitate [their leaders]. They are drowning in the darknesses of ignorance, like someone who is drowning under the waves that exist within the deep sea. Above the darkness of this lower wave is the darkness of a higher wave, and above that is the darkness of the clouds. This illustrates the intensity of the darkness in which the disbelievers are in. Hence, the heart of the disbeliever suffers from severe darkness and estrangement. The Most High said, **"And he to whom Allah has not granted light – for him there is no light."** [an-Noor (24): 40] For that reason, the Messenger of Allah ﷺ used to say, ***"Allâhumma Ij'al Fee Qalby Noorâ, wa Fee Basary Noorâ, wa Fee Sam'y Noorâ, wa 'An Yameeny Noorâ, wa 'An Yasâry Noorâ, wa Fawqy Noorâ, wa Tahty Noorâ, wa Amâmy Noorâ, wa Khalfy Noorâ, wa A'dhim Ly Noorâ*** (O Allah, place in my heart a light, and in my eyesight a light, and in my hearing a light, and on

The first (no. 39) is an example for the corrupt beliefs and the actions that result from them. One considers them to be of benefit to him, but upon approaching them he does not find anything of benefit to him, and then Allah repays him for those actions.[1] The second (no. 40) is an example for simple ignorance, and the absence of *eemân* and knowledge. Its victim is surrounded by darknesses, some of them atop others, wherein he cannot see anything since [true] vision is only with the light of *eemân* and knowledge.

The Most High said,

$$ \text{إِنَّ الَّذِينَ اتَّقَوْا إِذَا مَسَّهُمْ طَائِفٌ مِّنَ الشَّيْطَانِ تَذَكَّرُوا فَإِذَا هُم مُّبْصِرُونَ} $$

Indeed, those who fear [Allah] – when an impulse touches them from Satan, they remember [Him] and at once they have insight.[2] [al-A'râf (7): 201]

$$ \text{وَلَقَدْ هَمَّتْ بِهِ وَهَمَّ بِهَا لَوْلَا أَن رَّأَى بُرْهَانَ رَبِّهِ} $$

---

my right a light, and on my left a light, and above me a light, and below me a light, and in front of me a light, and behind me a light, and make great for me [my] light)." [Narrated by Muslim (763), Abu Dâwud (1353), and an-Nasâ'i (1121)]

[1] Just as Allah ﷻ said about them, **"[Some] faces, that Day, will be humbled. Working [hard] and exhausted."** [al-Ghâshiya (88): 2-3] They work and exhaust themselves in performing deeds that they hope will benefit them, just like the thirsty person who is hopeful that he will find water at the mirage. Similarly, you find Christian priests who sometimes boast that they remained for lengthy years without allowing water to come in contact with their bodies. He thinks this to be a righteous act that will benefit him, when it is actually the complete opposite. This is according to one of the interpretations of this verse, which holds that the **"exhausting work"** is what happens in this worldly life. The other interpretation is that it happens on the Day of Resurrection, when he experiences the most intense exhaustion, and is subjected to actions in the Fire through which he is tortured.

This verse also contains a scientific miracle, for it establishes that underwater waves exist below the waves that are observable on the oceanic surface.

[2] With the light of knowledge and *eemân*, he has the insight to discern truth from falsehood and guidance from deviance.

And she certainly sought him, and he would have sought her – had he not seen the proof of his Lord.[1] [Yoosuf (12): 24]

This proof was the *eemân* that manifested in his heart. Because of it, Allah removed what he [initially] sought, wrote a complete good deed for him, and did not write a bad deed against him – for he performed a good deed, and did not commit any sin.

The Most High said,

$$لِتُخْرِجَ النَّاسَ مِنَ الظُّلُمَاتِ إِلَى النُّورِ$$

...that you [O Muhammad] may bring people out from the darknesses into the light.

[Ibrâheem (14): 1]

$$اللَّهُ وَلِيُّ الَّذِينَ آمَنُوا يُخْرِجُهُم مِّنَ الظُّلُمَاتِ إِلَى النُّورِ وَالَّذِينَ كَفَرُوا أَوْلِيَاؤُهُمُ الطَّاغُوتُ يُخْرِجُونَهُم مِّنَ النُّورِ إِلَى الظُّلُمَاتِ$$

Allah is the Guardian of those who believe. He brings them out from darknesses into the light. And those who disbelieve – their allies are the false gods. They take them out from the light into darknesses. [al-Baqara (2): 257]

---

[1] The "seeking" done by the wife of al-'Azeez was not void of pursuit. Rather, she sought and pursued him, and that is called resolve or determination. She was not prevented from that by the fear of Allah ﷻ. Rather, the only thing that prevented her was the fleeing of Yoosuf ﷺ from her, and her finding her husband at the door. As for the "seeking" of Yoosuf ﷺ, it was void of pursuit, and that is called an insinuation. This type of "seeking" is not written as a sin, so long as there is no resolve to act upon it. Rather, a good deed is written when this "seeking" is left due to the fear of Allah ﷻ, just as the Prophet ﷺ said, **"Whoever seeks to perform a good deed, but does not perform it, a good deed is written for him. And whoever seeks to perform a good deed, and then performs it, ten to seven hundred fold [its reward] is written for him. And whoever seeks to perform an evil deed, but does not perform it, it is not written [against him]. And if he performs it, then it is written [against him]."** [Narrated by Muslim (130) and Ahmad (2519)]

$$\text{يَا أَيُّهَا الَّذِينَ آمَنُوا اتَّقُوا اللَّهَ وَآمِنُوا بِرَسُولِهِ يُؤْتِكُمْ كِفْلَيْنِ مِن رَّحْمَتِهِ وَيَجْعَل لَّكُمْ نُورًا تَمْشُونَ بِهِ}$$

O you who have believed, fear Allah and believe in His Messenger; He will [then] give you a double portion of His mercy and make for you a light by which you will walk. [al-Ḥadeed (57): 28]

For this reason, Allah struck two examples for the believers; an example with the water, which sustains life, and the scum that comes with it, and an example with the fire, which generates light, and the scum that comes with that which boils upon it. Likewise, Allah struck two examples for the hypocrites. The Most High said [regarding the believers],

$$\text{أَنزَلَ مِنَ السَّمَاءِ مَاءً فَسَالَتْ أَوْدِيَةٌ بِقَدَرِهَا فَاحْتَمَلَ السَّيْلُ زَبَدًا رَّابِيًا وَمِمَّا يُوقِدُونَ عَلَيْهِ فِي النَّارِ ابْتِغَاءَ حِلْيَةٍ أَوْ مَتَاعٍ زَبَدٌ مِّثْلُهُ كَذَلِكَ يَضْرِبُ اللَّهُ الْحَقَّ وَالْبَاطِلَ فَأَمَّا الزَّبَدُ فَيَذْهَبُ جُفَاءً وَأَمَّا مَا يَنفَعُ النَّاسَ فَيَمْكُثُ فِي الْأَرْضِ كَذَلِكَ يَضْرِبُ اللَّهُ الْأَمْثَالَ}$$

He sends down rain from the sky, and valleys flow according to their capacity, and the torrent carries rising scum. And from that [ore] which they heat in the fire, desiring adornments and utensils, is scum like it. Thus Allah presents [the example of] truth and falsehood. As for the scum, it vanishes, [being] cast off; but as for that which benefits the people, it remains on the earth. In this manner, Allah presents the examples.[1] [ar-Ra'd (13): 17]

---

[1] In this verse, Allah ﷻ strikes two examples for truth and falsehood in the hearts of the believers. In the first example, the Most High said, **"He sends down from the sky,**

rain…" This is the revealed truth which He sent down upon His Messenger 靏, "…and valleys flow according to their capacity." Each valley filled with water, and it flowed therein, to the degree of its size. The wide valley had much water flow into it, and the tight valley had little water flow into it. The hearts are like valleys; each of them fills with knowledge, *eemân*, and righteous deeds, but in varying proportions. "And the torrent carries rising scum," meaning the flowing water picks up grass and its likes, and they rise onto the water's surface. This is the example of the falsehood that mixes with the truth in a believer's heart, such as sins and the likes, whereby the pure, clean water is the primary substance and the scum is adventitious.

Then, Allah 靏 struck another example, and said, "And from that [ore] which they heat in the fire, desiring adornments and utensils, is scum like it." In other words, the metals that are smelted to become adornment – like gold and silver – or to become utensils – like iron and brass – also become mixed with impure, extraneous materials, and must enter the forge in order to be purified. This is an example of the truth and falsehood in the heart of a believer; it is like the metals that are mixed with impurities.

The first example was struck for the hearts of the purest slaves. The *eemân* in their hearts is the primary element, the scum is incidental, and it quickly disappears. As for the *eemân* in the fiery example, it is mixed with impurities to begin with, and requires various forms of trials and tribulations in order to become cleansed and purified, for its scum does not easily disappear.

Allah 靏 made the hearts of His slaves to be various types. Of them are those disposed upon the truth, and when falsehood visits such a heart, it quickly departs. Of them are those disposed on other than that, and for that reason he requires a greater effort to rectify himself. Thus, he 靏 said to al-Ashajj ibn 'Abd Qays, "Verily, in you are two qualities that Allah loves; *hilm* (forbearance) and *anâh* (deliberation)." [Narrated by Muslim (17), at-Tirmidhi (2011), and Ibn Mâjah (4188)] Some people are predisposed upon forbearance and deliberation, while others are inherently hasty and quick to anger, and so the latter requires a greater effort to rectify and refine himself, just as he 靏 said, "Knowledge is but by learning, and forbearance is but by practicing forbearance. Whoever pursues good will be granted it, and whoever avoids evil will be shielded from it." [Narrated by ad-Dâraqutni in *al-Afrâd* and deemed *hasan* by al-Albâni in *Saheeh al-Jâmi'* (2328)] Just as the minds of humanity vary, whereby there is the intelligent and the less intelligent, the hearts and character traits vary as well. We don't say to the less intelligent, "Don't learn," but rather we say to him, "Learn and strive as best you can." Likewise, there are those whom Allah 靏 disposed upon bravery, generosity, knowledge, or any other beautiful quality, and there are those who are not like this, and hence they must strive to refine themselves and acquire these beautiful qualities. We are not to say there is no benefit in trying to refine ourselves, rather these efforts are like the fire and forge; it removes the falsehood from the heart. The Most High said, "As for the scum, it vanishes, [being] cast off…" It is all eliminated; the scum atop the water is cast to the sides of the valley by the current and continues on its way, and the scum in the metals rises to its surface upon heating and is removed.

The Most High said, "And as for that which benefits the people, it remains on the earth." That which benefits the people of water, gold, silver, and various metals,

Regarding the hypocrites, the Most High said,

مَثَلُهُمْ كَمَثَلِ الَّذِي اسْتَوْقَدَ نَارًا فَلَمَّا أَضَاءَتْ مَا حَوْلَهُ ذَهَبَ اللَّهُ بِنُورِهِمْ وَتَرَكَهُمْ فِي ظُلُمَاتٍ لَا يُبْصِرُونَ ۞ صُمٌّ بُكْمٌ عُمْيٌ فَهُمْ لَا يَرْجِعُونَ ۞ أَوْ كَصَيِّبٍ مِنَ السَّمَاءِ فِيهِ ظُلُمَاتٌ وَرَعْدٌ وَبَرْقٌ يَجْعَلُونَ أَصَابِعَهُمْ فِي آذَانِهِمْ مِنَ الصَّوَاعِقِ حَذَرَ الْمَوْتِ ۞ وَاللَّهُ مُحِيطٌ بِالْكَافِرِينَ ۞ يَكَادُ الْبَرْقُ يَخْطَفُ أَبْصَارَهُمْ ۞ كُلَّمَا أَضَاءَ لَهُم مَّشَوْا فِيهِ وَإِذَا أَظْلَمَ عَلَيْهِمْ قَامُوا ۞ وَلَوْ شَاءَ اللَّهُ لَذَهَبَ بِسَمْعِهِمْ وَأَبْصَارِهِمْ ۞ إِنَّ اللَّهَ عَلَى كُلِّ شَيْءٍ قَدِيرٌ

Their example is that of one who kindled a fire, but when it illuminated what was around him, Allah took away their light and left them in darkness [so] they could not see. Deaf, dumb and blind - so they will not return [to the right path]. Or [it is] like a rainstorm from the sky within which is darkness, thunder, and lightning. They put their fingers in their ears against the thunderclaps in dread of death. But Allah is encompassing of the disbelievers. The lightning almost snatches away their sight. Every time it lights [the way] for them, they walk therein; but when darkness comes

---

all remain in the end after the scum has vanished. This is what infuses the believers with a feeling of reassurance, for every scum and falsehood they confront will eventually vanish, and their only duty is to remain committed to eemân and righteous deeds. So if we want our [good] deeds and da'wah to continue, we must firmly grip onto the revelation that descended from Allah, and become cleansed from the scum and falsehood that entered upon us from the outside, or existed within us to begin with. Hence, it's an absolute must that we clean and rectify our hearts.

over them, they stand [still]. And if Allah had willed, He could have taken away their hearing and their sight. Indeed, Allah is over all things capable.[1] [al-Baqara (2): 17-20]

Regarding them, the [first] example was struck of someone who kindled a fire, but whenever it illuminated, Allah extinguished it. The [second] example was that of water, which descends from the sky, but it came with darknesses, thunder, and lightning which allows visibility. The detailed explanation of these examples belongs elsewhere, whereas the objective here is to allude to the light of the hearts and their illumination.

---

[1] Here, Allah ﷻ strikes two examples for the hypocrites. In the first example, the Most High said, **"Their example is that of one who kindled a fire,"** meaning to see truth from falsehood. **"But when it illuminated what was around him, Allah took away their light."** When Allah saw what their hearts contained of pollution, He removed the light with which they used to distinguish truth from falsehood, **"and left them in darkness [so] they could not see."** This is the example of those who believed and then became hypocrites; may Allah protect us. Allah ﷻ did not mention that he removed from them the smoke or heat of the fire, but rather only mentioned the removal of their light. In that is an indication that the smoke and fire remained with them - meaning the torment and grief that comes with disbelief and hypocrisy. The Most High then said, **"Deaf, dumb, and blind – so they will not return [to the right path]."** They are deaf to hearing the truth, mute in terms of speaking the truth, blind to seeing the truth, and therefore they will not return back from their hypocrisy. The phrase **"so they will not return"** supports the view of those who said this verse was revealed about people who initially believed and later became hypocrites. The Most High then struck another example for the hypocrites by saying, **"Or [it is] like a rainstorm from the sky within which is darkness, thunder, and lightning. They put their fingers in their ears against the thunderclaps in dread of death… The lightning almost snatches away their sight. Every time it lights [the way] for them, they walk therein; but when darkness comes over them, they stand [still]."** In other words, this type of hypocrite is like a man caught in the rain - rain accompanied by darkness, lightning, and thunder. This refers to the various types of confusions and doubts that the hypocrite experiences regarding the truth that Allah revealed. It came down to bring life to the hearts, just as the rain gives life to the earth, but due to their misguidance and ignorance, they were afflicted with doubts by it instead. The thunder refers to the fear which rattles their hearts, and the lightning refers to the glimmer of faith that sometimes flashes in the hearts of these hypocrites. **"Every time it lights [the way] for them, they walk therein,"** meaning every time an aspect of faith appears before them, they are comforted by it and follow it. **"But when darkness comes over them, they stand [still]."** In other words, there are times when the darkness of doubt presents itself, darkening their hearts and causing them to stop from bewilderment. The example of fire was struck for the pure hypocrites, and the example of water was struck for those with doubts and confusion.

There occurs in the narration [prophetic] supplication, **"Make the Qur'an the rabee' (nourishment) of our hearts, and the light of our chests."**[1] The *rabee'* is the rain which descends from the sky and causes the vegetation to sprout.[2] The Prophet 🕌 said, **"Indeed, of that which the *rabee'* causes to sprout kills or nearly [kills]."**[3][4] The season when the first rainfall descends was named *ar-Rabee'* (Spring) by the Arabs due to the rain that falls during it and produces vegetation, and others gave the name *ar-Rabee'* to the season following winter (pre-Spring), for in it the flowers blossom to [later] develop into fruits, and the leaves begin growing on the trees.

Due to the light it contains, this alive and illuminated heart hears, sees, and understands. As for the dead heart, it neither hears nor sees. The Most High said,

$$وَمَثَلُ الَّذِينَ كَفَرُوا كَمَثَلِ الَّذِي يَنْعِقُ بِمَا لَا يَسْمَعُ إِلَّا دُعَاءً وَنِدَاءً صُمٌّ بُكْمٌ عُمْيٌ فَهُمْ لَا يَعْقِلُونَ$$

The example of those who disbelieve is like that of someone who shouts at what hears nothing but calls and cries (i.e. cattle or sheep); deaf, dumb and blind, so they do not understand.[5] [al-Baqara (2): 171]

---

[1] Collected by Aḥmad (1877), Ibn Ḥibbân (972), aṭ-Ṭabarâni in *al-Kabeer* (270, 10352), and al-Albâni deemed it authentic in *Ṣaḥeeḥ at-Targheeb wat-Tarheeb* (1822).
[2] The Qur'an [acts] in the hearts like the rain of springtime, which causes the earth to sprout and come to life. Likewise, the Qur'an causes goodness to sprout in the hearts. So this hadith combined between "life" which involves activity and growth, and between "light" which is knowledge, and perceiving things as they truly are.
[3] Collected by Muslim (1052), Ibn Mâjah (3995), and Ibn Ḥibbân (3227).
[4] His words 🕌, **"that which kills,"** refers [in the Arabic] to the animal which dies from overeating. His words 🕌, **"or nearly,"** means it almost kills. The point being is that worldly good could increase until it becomes evil for its possessor, causing him to fall sick or perhaps even die.
[5] The example of the disbelievers, with regards to the call of the Qur'an, is like that of the animal which the shepherd calls out to with his voice. These grazing animals do not understand this call, nor make any sense of it, nor consider it to be anything except a mere sound. The Most High said, **"Deaf, dumb, and blind – so they do not understand."** Allah 🕋 only afflicted them with this deafness, dumbness, and blindness, because they turned away from the truth.

وَمِنْهُم مَّن يَسْتَمِعُونَ إِلَيْكَ أَفَأَنتَ تُسْمِعُ الصُّمَّ وَلَوْ كَانُوا لَا يَعْقِلُونَ ۝ وَمِنْهُم مَّن يَنظُرُ
إِلَيْكَ أَفَأَنتَ تَهْدِي الْعُمْيَ وَلَوْ كَانُوا لَا يُبْصِرُونَ

And among them are those who listen to you. But can you cause the deaf to hear, although they will not use reason? And among them are those who look at you. But can you guide the blind although they will not [attempt to] see?[1] [Yoonus (10): 42-43]

وَمِنْهُم مَّن يَسْتَمِعُ إِلَيْكَ وَجَعَلْنَا عَلَىٰ قُلُوبِهِمْ أَكِنَّةً أَن يَفْقَهُوهُ وَفِي آذَانِهِمْ وَقْرًا وَإِن يَرَوْا
كُلَّ آيَةٍ لَّا يُؤْمِنُوا بِهَا حَتَّىٰ إِذَا جَاءُوكَ يُجَادِلُونَكَ يَقُولُ الَّذِينَ كَفَرُوا إِنْ هَٰذَا إِلَّا أَسَاطِيرُ
الْأَوَّلِينَ

And among them are those who listen to you, but We have placed over their hearts coverings, lest they understand it, and in their ears deafness. And if they should see every sign, they will not believe in it. Even when they come to you arguing with you, those who disbelieve say: "This is not but legends of the former peoples."[2] [al-Anʿâm (6): 25]

---

[1] So the disbelievers have hearing, sight, and senses by which they can understand their worldly affairs. However, after the proofs were established against them, and they turned away from the truth, they became deaf whereby they could no longer hear or understand the truth, and became blind whereby they could no longer recognize the guidance.

[2] His words, **"over their hearts coverings,"** means upon them are covers whereby they cannot understand the Qurʾan. His words, **"and in their ears deafness,"** mean heavy hearing, whereby it's as if they don't hear the Qurʾan. **"And if they should see every sign, they would not believe in it,"** meaning despite the signs being as clear as the sun. This is all a punishment from Allah ﷻ because they didn't believe in it the first time.

Here, He ﷻ informed that they do not understand with their hearts, nor hear with their ears, nor believe in the Fire which they have seen, just as He ﷻ informed about them saying,

وَقَالُوا قُلُوبُنَا فِي أَكِنَّةٍ مِّمَّا تَدْعُونَا إِلَيْهِ وَفِي آذَانِنَا وَقْرٌ وَمِن بَيْنِنَا وَبَيْنِكَ حِجَابٌ

And they say, "Our hearts are within coverings from that to which you invite us, in our ears is deafness, and between us and you is a partition."[1] [Fuṣṣilat (41): 5]

They mentioned the impediments upon the hearts, hearings, and sights – even though their bodies were alive and able to hear sounds and see individuals – but the life of the body, without the life of the heart, is identical to the life of the beasts; they have hearing and sight, and they eat, drink, and copulate. For this reason, the Most High said, **"The example of those who disbelieve is like that of one who shouts at what hears nothing but calls and cries."** [al-Baqara (2): 171] He compared them to the sheep that the shepherd shouts at, while they hear nothing but [unintelligible] calls and cries, just as He said in the other verses,

أَمْ تَحْسَبُ أَنَّ أَكْثَرَهُمْ يَسْمَعُونَ أَوْ يَعْقِلُونَ إِنْ هُمْ إِلَّا كَالْأَنْعَامِ بَلْ هُمْ أَضَلُّ سَبِيلًا

Or do you think that most of them hear or reason? They are not except like livestock. Rather, they are [even] more astray in [their] way. [al-Furqân (25): 44]

وَلَقَدْ ذَرَأْنَا لِجَهَنَّمَ كَثِيرًا مِّنَ الْجِنِّ وَالْإِنسِ لَهُمْ قُلُوبٌ لَّا يَفْقَهُونَ بِهَا وَلَهُمْ أَعْيُنٌ لَّا يُبْصِرُونَ بِهَا وَلَهُمْ آذَانٌ لَّا يَسْمَعُونَ بِهَا أُولَٰئِكَ كَالْأَنْعَامِ بَلْ هُمْ أَضَلُّ

---

[1] They had said this in mockery and stubbornness. In other words, whatever you do – we will not believe in you. Or, this could be them citing destiny as evidence, whereby they are blaming their rejection of the Messenger ﷺ on fate.

And We have certainly created for Hell many of the jinn and mankind. They have
hearts with which they do not understand, they have eyes with which they do not see,
and they have ears with which they do not hear. Those are like livestock; rather, they
are more astray. [al-A'râf (7): 179]

A group of [Qur'anic] interpreters, with regards to the likes of these verses,

$$وَإِذَا مَسَّ الْإِنسَانَ الضُّرُّ دَعَانَا لِجَنبِهِ أَوْ قَاعِدًا أَوْ قَائِمًا فَلَمَّا كَشَفْنَا عَنْهُ ضُرَّهُ مَرَّ كَأَن$$

$$لَّمْ يَدْعُنَا إِلَىٰ ضُرٍّ مَّسَّهُ$$

And when affliction touches the human being, he calls upon Us, whether lying on his
side or sitting or standing; but when We remove from him his affliction, he continues
[in disobedience] as if he had never called upon Us to [remove] an affliction that
touched him. [Yoonus (10): 12]

...and their likes wherein Allah mentions and dispraises the flaws of humans, they
say, "This verse refers to the disbelievers, and the intended human being here is the
disbeliever." As a result, those who hear this assume that the claimants to Islam have no share
of this dispraise and threat. Instead, their imagination wanders to the Arabs that profess
polytheism, or to those they know to openly profess disbelief, such as the Jews, Christians,
the polytheists among the Turks and Indians, and the likes. Consequently, they do not benefit
from these verses that Allah sent down for the guidance of His slaves.

Firstly, what should be said is that those who profess Islam include the believer and
the hypocrite, and the hypocrites are plenty in every age, and the hypocrites are in the lowest
pit of the Hellfire.

Secondly, it must be said that a human being may contain a branch of hypocrisy or
disbelief, even if they possess *eemân*, just as the Prophet ﷺ said in the agreed upon hadith,
"Four [qualities] — whoever possesses them is a complete hypocrite, and whoever

possesses a quality of them possesses a quality of hypocrisy until he abandons it; he lies when he speaks, he betrays when he is trusted, he breaks when he promises, and he is vulgar when he disputes."[1] Here, he informed that whoever possesses one of these qualities possesses a quality of hypocrisy. Likewise, it has been confirmed in the authentic hadith that he ﷺ said to Abu Dharr ﵁, **"You are a man in whom is *Jâhiliyya*."**[2] – even though Abu Dharr is of the most genuine people in *eemân*. As well, he ﷺ said in the authentic hadith, **"Four [qualities] in my *ummah* that are from the affairs of *Jâhiliyya*: boasting about ancestry, slandering lineages, wailing, and seeking rain through the stars."**[3] As well, he ﷺ said in the authentic hadith, **"You will surely follow the ways of those before you, step by step, even if they enter a lizard's hole – you will surely enter it."** They said, "The Jews and Christians?" He said, **"Who else?"**[4] He ﷺ also said in the authentic hadith, **"My nation will surely indulge just as the nations before it indulged, hand span by hand span, and arm's length by arm's length."** They said, "Persia and Rome?" He said, "Who else but them?"[5]

Ibn Abi Mulayka said, "I met thirty of the companions of Muhammad ﷺ; each of them fearing hypocrisy for himself."[6] Similarly, on the authority of 'Ali ﵁ – or Hudhayfa ﵁ – who said, "The hearts are four [types]: a clear heart that contains a glowing torch – that being the heart of the believer, an encased heart[7] – that being the heart of the disbeliever,

---

[1] Narrated by al-Bukhâri (34) and Muslim (59).
[2] Narrated by al-Bukhâri (30) and Muslim (1661).
[3] Narrated by Muslim (934).
[4] Narrated by al-Bukhâri (3456).
[5] Narrated by al-Bukhâri (7319).
[6] The likes of these verses were revealed about all people, but with varying degrees. Certainly, they primarily refer to the disbelievers and apply to them completely. As well, the hypocrites guilty of major hypocrisy, who claim to be Muslim but are actually disbelievers; these verses are about them as well. As for the believers who possess some minor hypocrisy, they have a share of the address found in these verses. You find many people – due to their deficiency in *eemân* – hearing these verses and not understanding them, nor responding to them, and in that they bear a resemblance of the disbelievers about whom these verses were originally revealed.
[7] Meaning, it is covered, and this prevents *eemân* from entering it.

an overturned heart[1] – that being the heart of the hypocrite, and a heart with two fuels; a fuel that supplies it with *eemân* and a fuel that supplies it with hypocrisy – these being people who mixed good acts with others that are evil."[2]

VI – The Straight Path

Once this has been understood, it becomes evident that every slave benefits from what Allah mentions concerning *eemân*, whether of praising the branches of *eemân* or dispraising the branches of disbelief. This is similar to what some have discussed about His words,

$$اهْدِنَا الصِّرَاطَ الْمُسْتَقِيمَ$$

Guide us [to] the straight path. [al-Fâtiḥah (1): 6]

They said, "The believer has already been guided to the straight path, so what is gained by requesting guidance?!" Some [scholars] responded that the intended meaning was, "Keep us firm upon the guidance," just as the Arabs would say to someone [already] sleeping, "Sleep until I reach you." Others said, "Lock our hearts upon guidance," whereby the literal [meaning] was omitted. Others said, "Increase me in guidance." This question was only posed by them because of their inability to [correctly] perceive this straight path, which the slave requests guidance towards. Its actual meaning is to act upon what Allah commanded, and to abandon what Allah forbid, in all matters.

Even if a person holistically affirms that Muhammad is the Messenger of Allah, and that the Qur'an is the truth – most of the knowledge he needs regarding what benefits and

---

[1] Meaning, like a container that was flipped, whereby nothing can remain inside. Such is the hypocrite; goodness does not remain in him.

[2] The point being is that people are not all disbelievers, but rather among them are hypocrites, and among them are those who have some of the qualities of the disbelievers and hypocrites.

harms him, and what he was commanded with and prohibited from, in the specific detailed matters remains unknown by him[1]. Even what he knows, much of it he has not acted upon[2]. Even if every command and prohibition in the Qur'an and Sunnah were to reach him – the Qur'an and Sunnah only contain mention of the general, overall matters. Anything else is impossible; and thus it does not mention what is particular to each slave[3]. Thus, the slave was commanded to request guidance to the straight path in light of these factors.

Guidance to the straight path incorporates all of this. It includes knowing what the Messenger brought in detail, knowing what falls under his general commands, and being inspired to act upon one's knowledge. This is because simply knowing the truth does not entail guidance if one does not act upon his knowledge, and for this reason, He ﷻ said to His Prophet after the Treaty of al-Ḥudaybiya,

$$ إِنَّا فَتَحْنَا لَكَ فَتْحًا مُّبِينًا ۝ لِّيَغْفِرَ لَكَ اللَّهُ مَا تَقَدَّمَ مِن ذَنبِكَ وَمَا تَأَخَّرَ وَيُتِمَّ نِعْمَتَهُ عَلَيْكَ وَيَهْدِيَكَ صِرَاطًا مُّسْتَقِيمًا $$

---

[1] Therefore, a component of *eemân* is holistic, and a component is detailed. Knowing the straight path is by getting to know the details of *eemân* after generally believing in it.

[2] Indeed, how many people know the truth and do not conform to it. Hence, guidance to the straight path is by knowledge and actions, of both the general and the detailed matters.

[3] This is because every slave is subjected to detailed circumstances that he needs to know the Sharia ruling for, and it is impossible that the Qur'an and Sunnah specifically address every single situation the slave could ever experience. The Qur'an and *Sunnah*, for instance, mentioned that *ribâ* (interest) is unlawful, and you find yourself presented with money that you wish to take, but do not know whether this is *ribâ* or not. This is a detailed situation which you measure against the general ruling regarding the prohibition of *ribâ*. Hence, the straight path incorporates many details, and it requires being guided in terms of knowledge at large, and then its details pertaining to every specific incident. Then, it requires being guided in terms of will-power and actions, so that one loves the truth, seeks it, intends to perform it, then actually practices it, and then remains steadfast and committed to it until he meets Allah while safe from that which would nullify those actions.

Indeed, We have given you [O Muhammad] a clear conquest. That Allah may forgive for you what preceded of your sin, and what will follow, and to complete His favor upon you and guide you to a straight path.[1] [al-Fath (48): 1-2]

As well, He ﷻ said regarding Moosâ and Hâroon,

$$وَآتَيْنَاهُمَا الْكِتَابَ الْمُسْتَبِينَ ۝ وَهَدَيْنَاهُمَا الصِّرَاطَ الْمُسْتَقِيمَ$$

And We gave them the explicit scripture. And We guided them on the straight path.
[as-Sâffât (37): 117-118]

The Muslims have disputed over whatever Allah willed of the informational, theoretical, theological, and practical matters despite them all agreeing that Muhammad was true, and the Qur'an being truth. Had they all been guided to the straight path regarding what they differed over, they would not have differed[2]. Additionally, those who knew what Allah commanded – most of them disobey Him and do not follow His instruction. Had they been guided to the straight path with regards to these actions, they would have done what they were commanded and abstained from what they were forbidden. As for those from this Ummah whom Allah guided until they became from amongst the pious *awliyâ'* of Allah, one of the greatest reasons for that was their supplicating to Allah with this supplication in every prayer, alongside their knowing that they have a dire need for Allah to guide them to the straight path at all times.

---

[1] The treaty that took place on the Day of al-Hudaybiya, despite the unjust conditions that were stipulated by the polytheists, was actually good and an [eventual] conquest to which Allah had guided His Messenger ﷺ. Therefore, this was of the guidance of Allah ﷻ for His Messenger ﷺ, which indicates that guidance is needed by every person, even if he were to reach the highest stations.

[2] The disagreements among the people of Islam, and the existence of the people of deviance and innovation amidst them, prove that not every Muslim has been guided to the straight path in both the general and specific matters. They all agree, in general, that the Messenger is true and that the Qur'an is true, but disagreed thereafter in the details.

Therefore, it was by their consistency in this supplication, and their acknowledging their poverty [for Allah], that they became of the pious *awliyā'* of Allah. Sahl b. 'Abdillāh at-Tustari said, "There is no route between the slave and his Lord faster than acknowledging [one's] poverty."

What one has attained guidance for previously, he still needs to attain guidance for it in the future, and this is the reality behind the statement of those who said, "Keep us firm, and guide us to remain upon the path."[1] For this reason, Allah obligated it upon them in every prayer, for there is no supplication that they have a greater need for than this.

The statement of those who said, "Increase us in guidance," also falls under the aforementioned. However, these [interpretations] are all referring to being guided in the future to the straight path, for acting upon the knowledge in the future has not yet happened, and he will not be guided until he acts in the future upon his knowledge. In fact, he may not attain the knowledge in the future [to begin with], or it could even leave his heart [after attainment], or it could be attained but the actions are not. Therefore, the people are all direly in need of this supplication, and once guidance is granted to the straight path, then victory, sustenance, and every delight which the souls seek is attained. And Allah knows best.

VII – The Reality of the Heart's Life

Know that the heart's life, like the life of others, is not merely the [faculty of] sensing and moving voluntarily, nor is it merely knowledge and power – as some theoreticians, like Abu al-Husayn al-Basri, have presumed regarding the knowledge and power of Allah. They said: "His life lies in that He knows and is capable." No, rather life is a distinct quality in whatever is being described, and it is a prerequisite for knowledge, will-

---

[1] Therefore, guidance to the straight path includes knowledge and actions in both the general and the specific. Then, it requires being steadfast upon this knowledge and action, and that is the meaning of the view which says, **"Guide us [to] the straight path,"** means keep us firm and guide us to staying committed to the path. Indeed, for there are some people who give up righteous actions after having once been consistent upon them, and therefore a person needs steadfastness upon the straight path for the future as well.

power, and the ability to perform actions voluntarily. As well, it necessitates all of that. Hence, everything living has feelings, will-power, and the ability to act at will – and everything that has knowledge, will-power, and voluntary actions is alive.

Hayâ' (Shame) is derived from *hayâh* (life), because the person with a living heart is alive, and his shame prevents him from indecency – for the heart's life is its immunity against the indecencies that corrupt the heart. For this reason, the Prophet ﷺ said, **"*Hayâ'* is from eemân."**[1] He ﷺ also said, **"*Hayâ'* and bafflement are two branches of eemân, while vulgarity and eloquence are two branches of hypocrisy."**[2][3] This is because the living wards off what harms him, while the dead is lifeless and thus is called *waqih* (impudent). *Waqâha* is rigidity, that of the dry ground, which is contrary to the moisture of life[4]. So if someone is impudent, rigid, and stone faced, then there is no life in his heart to make him

---

[1] Narrated by al-Bukhâri (24) and Muslim (39).

[2] Narrated by at-Tirmidhi (2113) and deemed authentic by al-Albâni.

[3] Here, **"bafflement"** is referring to the inability to play with words, whereby he informs of matters as they truly are. He does not present the falsehood as truth, or the truth as falsehood. As for the **"eloquence"** intended here, that is referring to the person who decorates falsehood and depicts it to the people as truth, or the opposite. Such has been described by the Messenger ﷺ as a branch of hypocrisy, and this is the **"articulation"** about which he ﷺ said, **"Indeed, in *bayân* (clear articulation) there is [the effect of] sorcery."** [Narrated by Abu Dâwud (5007) and deemed authentic by al-Albâni] This is also the "persuasiveness" about which he ﷺ said, **"...and perhaps some of you are *alhan* (more persuasive) than others."** [Narrated by al-Bukhâri (2680) and Muslim (1713)] An example of this is a lawyer who presents the criminal as innocent while he in reality is a criminal. This is the eloquence and articulation which is a branch of hypocrisy, and not just any eloquent speech, since the Messenger ﷺ was named by Allah a *"mubeen"* Messenger, meaning he *yubayyin* (clarifies) truth from falsehood to the people using a clear and comprehendible style. This has nothing to do with hypocrisy – may Allah forbid – but rather is a quality of the Messenger ﷺ and a quality of his Companions ﷺ after him.

[4] For example, if we wanted to check a person's foot for disease or paralysis, we would poke him in the foot. If he moves it to escape what pains him, we would know that his leg isn't paralyzed, and that his leg remains "alive." But if he doesn't move it upon us poking him, this is an indication of the disease or paralysis of his foot, meaning there is a deficiency or absence of life in it. Likewise, the living heart feels bothered by evil and resists it; that is the essence of *hayâ'*. But when the heart lacks or is void of life, it isn't bothered by these harms and consequently does not resist them.

ashamed and prevent him from indecency. He is like the dry Earth that is unaffected by the feet stomping upon it, as oppose to the green Earth.

This is why the shameful person is noticeably bothered by indecency, and has the will-power that prevents him from performing indecent acts. As for the impudent, his lack of life results in him being void of shame, and lacking the *eemân* that deters from that.

If the heart is alive, and then the person dies by his soul exiting his body, its separation from the body is the bodily death, although the soul itself has not died in the sense that its life has terminated. For this reason, the Most High said,

$$وَلَا تَقُولُوا لِمَن يُقْتَلُ فِي سَبِيلِ اللَّهِ أَمْوَاتٌ بَلْ أَحْيَاءٌ$$

And do not say about those who are killed in the way of Allah, "They are dead." Rather, [they are] alive... [al-Baqara (2): 154]

$$وَلَا تَحْسَبَنَّ الَّذِينَ قُتِلُوا فِي سَبِيلِ اللَّهِ أَمْوَاتًا بَلْ أَحْيَاءٌ$$

And never think of those who have been killed in the cause of Allah as dead. Rather, [they are] alive... [Âli 'Imrân (3): 169]

...even though they are dead; falling under the statement of the Most High,

$$كُلُّ نَفْسٍ ذَائِقَةُ الْمَوْتِ$$

Every soul will taste death. [Âli 'Imrân (3): 185]

$$إِنَّكَ مَيِّتٌ وَإِنَّهُم مَّيِّتُونَ$$

Indeed, you are to die, and indeed, they are to die. [az-Zumar (39): 30]

$$\text{هُوَ الَّذِي أَحْيَاكُمْ ثُمَّ يُمِيتُكُمْ ثُمَّ يُحْيِيكُمْ}$$

And He is the one who gave you life; then He causes you to die and then will [again] give you life. [al-Ḥajj (22): 66]

Here, the death being affirmed differs from the death being negated. The affirmed is that of the soul departing the body, and the negated is that of life entirely leaving both the soul and body.

This is just like sleep being the brother of death; it is named both *wafāt* and *mawt* despite life existing during these states. Allah, the Most High, said,

$$\text{اللَّهُ يَتَوَفَّى الْأَنْفُسَ حِينَ مَوْتِهَا وَالَّتِي لَمْ تَمُتْ فِي مَنَامِهَا فَيُمْسِكُ الَّتِي قَضَى عَلَيْهَا}$$

$$\text{الْمَوْتَ وَيُرْسِلُ الْأُخْرَى إِلَى أَجَلٍ مُسَمًّى}$$

Allah takes the souls at the time of their death, and those that do not die [He takes] during their sleep. Then He keeps those for which He has decreed death and releases the others for a specified term. [az-Zumar (39): 42]

As well, when Prophet ﷺ used to awaken from sleeping, he would say: **"All praise be to Allah who gave us life, after putting us to death, and to Him is the [final] rising."**[1] In another hadith: **"All praise be to Allah who returned my soul to me, pardoned me in my body, permitted me to remember Him, and greatly preferred me over many of those He created."**[2] Also, when he would recline to his bed, he would say: **"O Allah! You created my soul, and you put it to death; for You is its living and its dying. If You withhold it, then have mercy on it, and if You send it, then safeguard it**

---

[1] Narrated by al-Bukhâri (6312) and Muslim (2711).
[2] Narrated by at-Tirmidhi (3641) with similar wording, and was deemed *ḥasan* by al-Albâni.

as You safeguard Your righteous slaves."[1] He ﷺ would also say, **"By your name, O Allah, I die and I live."**[2]

VIII – The Disease of Envy and its Types

Among the diseases of the hearts is *ḥasad* (envy). Some said regarding its definition, "A harm that results from knowing the excellent condition of the wealthy[3]." Based on that, a virtuous person cannot be envious, for the virtuous are pleased by excellence. Another group of people said, "Wishing that the blessing be removed from the envied[4], even if the envier does not acquire its likes[5]." This differs from *ghibṭa* (jealous admiration), for that denotes wishing its likes without liking that it be removed from the admired.

In essence, envy is the hatred of the excellent condition he notices in the envied, and it is of two types:

The first is hatred of the blessing [bestowed] upon him in the absolute sense, and this is the dispraised envy. And because he hates it, he will be pained and frustrated by the existence of what he hates. Such an individual is diseased at heart; his pleasure lies in the blessing leaving that [envied] person, even if its leaving does not accrue any benefit for him, although he does benefit by having the pains within him subsiding. However, the pain only subsided by his involvement [against it], which does comfort him, but its limit is like a sick person that is treated using what sedates his pain, though the disease remains. Likewise, his

---

[1] Narrated by al-Bukhâri (7393,6320) and Muslim (2714,2712).

[2] Narrated by al-Bukhâri (6314) with the wording, **"O Allah! By Your name, I die and I live,"** and Muslim (2711) with the wording: **"O Allah! By Your name I live, and by Your name I die."**

[3] This does not mean that the only envied person is he who is financially wealthy. Rather, he could be envied for being wealthy in terms of health or leadership, for just as the poor could be poor in terms of money, he could also be poor in terms of health, leadership, and otherwise. For example, imagine a sick person that has much wealth but is bankrupt in terms of health.

[4] This is the most famous position, and perhaps it is the closest to correctness.

[5] Therefore, there are several types of envy; to wish that the blessing would be removed from the envied and he would acquire it himself, and to wish that the blessing be removed, even if he will not acquire it himself.

hatred of the blessing that Allah bestows upon His slave is a disease, and this blessing could return to the envied, and even greater than it, just as the likes of this blessing could be bestowed upon the likes of this envied person[1].

This envier has no aim for anything specific, aside from his soul simply hating what others have been blessed with. For this reason, some said, "It is wishing that the blessing be removed," because whoever hates that another enjoys a blessing, he wishes for its removal at heart.

The second type is the hatred of that individual being preferred over him, whereby he loves to be equal or superior to him. This is [also] _hasad_ (envy), and is the one that they called _ghibta_. The Prophet ﷺ himself called it _hasad_ in the agreed upon hadith, on the authority of Ibn Mas'ood ﷺ and Ibn 'Umar ﷺ, wherein he said, **"There is no _hasad_ except in two: a man whom Allah granted wisdom, so he judges by it and teaches it, and a man whom Allah granted wealth, so he expended it all rightfully."**[2] This is the wording of Ibn Mas'ood. The wording of Ibn 'Umar, **"...a man whom Allah granted the Qur'an, so he upholds it by night and day, and a man whom Allah granted wealth, so he spends from it rightfully by night and day."**[3] It was also narrated by al-Bukhâri, on the authority of Abu Hurayra ﷺ, and its wording, **"There is no _hasad_ except in two: a man whom Allah granted the Qur'an, and he recites it by night and day, so a man hears him and says, 'O I wish I had been granted the likes of what he has been granted, so I may do with it the likes of what he does,' and a man whom Allah granted wealth, and he expends it rightfully, so a man says, 'O I wish I had been granted the likes of what he**

---

[1] It was for that reason that some said, "God bless envy; it kills its bearer first." The one who envies a person over a particular blessing only becomes happy when that blessing leaves him, but that happiness is temporary, and very quickly does the pain and grief in his heart increase. This is because the blessings of Allah upon His creation are abundant, and so he will see many more blessings being enjoyed by this person which he envied – which will frustrate him – and could even see that same blessing return to this person which he previously envied. As a result, he will live in pain and torment for his entire life, for the blessings of Allah upon His slaves do not stop. We seek refuge with Allah from envy.

[2] Narrated by al-Bukhâri (73) and Muslim (816).

[3] Narrated by al-Bukhâri (7529) and Muslim (815).

has been granted, so I may do with it the likes of what he does.'"[1] This *ḥasad*, which the Prophet ﷺ forbade except in [these] two scenarios, is what they called *ghibṭa*, and it refers to loving the condition of another and hating to be inferior to him.

If it were said: Why then was it called *ḥasad* when it is solely the love of being blessed by Allah? The response is that this love originates from him looking at His blessing of others, and him hating to be inferior to others. Were it not for the existence of this other, he would not have loved that. Therefore, since this began from his hatred of others being superior to him, it was deemed *ḥasad* – for it is hatred that resulted in love. As for someone who loves that Allah bestows His blessing upon him, without turning to the conditions of the people, this [person] is not envious whatsoever.

IX – *Ghibṭa* (Jealous Admiration)

Most people are afflicted with this second category, which is also called *munâfasa* (competition), whereby the two [individuals] compete with one another for a desired matter. Each of them seeks to take it, because of their hatred that the other surpasses them; just as each of the two racers hates that the other outraces him. Competition is not always dispraised; rather it is praiseworthy in [matters of] goodness. The Most High said,

إِنَّ الْأَبْرَارَ لَفِي نَعِيمٍ ۞ عَلَى الْأَرَائِكِ يَنظُرُونَ ۞ تَعْرِفُ فِي وُجُوهِهِمْ نَضْرَةَ النَّعِيمِ ۞ يُسْقَوْنَ مِن رَّحِيقٍ مَّخْتُومٍ ۞ خِتَامُهُ مِسْكٌ ۚ وَفِي ذَٰلِكَ فَلْيَتَنَافَسِ الْمُتَنَافِسُونَ

Indeed, the righteous will be in bliss. On adorned couches, observing. You will recognize in their faces the radiance of bliss. They will be given to drink [pure] wine [which was] sealed. The last of it is musk. So for this let the competitors compete. [al-Muṭaffifeen (83): 22-26]

---

[1] Narrated by al-Bukhâri (7232).

Here, He 🕮 instructed the competitors to compete in this bliss, and to not compete in the fleeting worldly enjoyment. This matches the hadith of the Prophet 🕮, for he forbade envy except of someone who was granted knowledge that he acts upon and teaches, and someone who was granted wealth that he spends. As for someone who was granted knowledge but did not act upon it nor teach it, or someone who was granted wealth but did not spend it in the obedience of Allah, then he should not be envied, nor should his condition be desired, for he is not upon any goodness worth aspiring for. In fact, he is subject to the punishment. As for someone who assumes a position of authority and serves it with knowledge and justice, delivers the trusts to their rightful owners, and judges between the people using the Qur'an and Sunnah – his degree is great, but such [a person] is in a great jihad (struggle).

Likewise is the *mujâhid* (combatant) in the way of Allah, and the souls do not envy someone in a great deal of adversity. For this reason, he did not mention him[1]. Even though the *mujâhid* in the way of Allah is superior to someone who spends [his] wealth, but not the spender and teacher, these two usually do not have an external enemy. Were they to have an enemy against which they struggle, that would better their degree [even further].

Similarly, the Prophet 🕮 did not mention the one who prays, the one who fasts, and the one who performs Hajj, because these actions usually do not benefit the people in ways that would make them exalt an individual and consider him a leader, as can be attained via teaching and spending. In origin, envy only results from the supremacy and leadership that occur to another. Aside from that, a worker is not usually envied, even if he is more blessed with regards to food, drink, and marriage than others. As for these two types, they are envied a great deal. For this reason, there exists more envy between the people of knowledge who have followers than there exists between those unlike them, and likewise with someone who has followers because of him spending his wealth. This one benefits the people by

---

[1] The Prophet 🕮 did not mention jihad along with knowledge and wealth – despite it also being a form of good – because the souls naturally lean to rest, and jihad involves much toil. Hence, the people envy those whom they assume are comforted, and don't envy those who undertake exhausting tasks.

nourishing their hearts, and that one benefits them by nourishing their bodies, and all people are in need of what benefits them of this and that.

That is why Allah ﷻ struck two examples – an example of this, and an example of that – by saying:

ضَرَبَ اللَّهُ مَثَلًا عَبْدًا مَّمْلُوكًا لَّا يَقْدِرُ عَلَىٰ شَيْءٍ وَمَن رَّزَقْنَاهُ مِنَّا رِزْقًا حَسَنًا فَهُوَ يُنفِقُ مِنْهُ سِرًّا وَجَهْرًا هَلْ يَسْتَوُونَ الْحَمْدُ لِلَّهِ بَلْ أَكْثَرُهُمْ لَا يَعْلَمُونَ ۝ وَضَرَبَ اللَّهُ مَثَلًا رَّجُلَيْنِ أَحَدُهُمَا أَبْكَمُ لَا يَقْدِرُ عَلَىٰ شَيْءٍ وَهُوَ كَلٌّ عَلَىٰ مَوْلَاهُ أَيْنَمَا يُوَجِّههُّ لَا يَأْتِ بِخَيْرٍ هَلْ يَسْتَوِي هُوَ وَمَن يَأْمُرُ بِالْعَدْلِ وَهُوَ عَلَىٰ صِرَاطٍ مُّسْتَقِيمٍ

Allah presents an example: a slave [who is] owned and unable to do a thing and he to whom We have provided from Us good provision, so he spends from it secretly and publicly. Can they be equal? Praise to Allah! But most of them do not know. And Allah presents an example of two men, one of them dumb and unable to do a thing, while he is a burden to his guardian. Wherever he directs him, he brings no good. Is he equal to one who commands justice, while he is on a straight path? [an-Naḥl (16): 75-76]

The two examples were struck by Allah ﷻ about His sublime Self, and about those worshipped beside Him[1] – for these idols are incapable of [performing] acts that benefit, nor [speaking] words that benefit. Imagine there was an owned slave that was

---

[1] These two examples were struck by Allah ﷻ regarding His blessed Self, to explain the incorrectness of worshipping other than Allah, whether that be idols or otherwise. There is another interpretation for these two examples, namely that this is the example of the believer and the disbeliever. The disbeliever is being resembled to the captive slave that possesses nothing, whereby he cannot grant or provide anything to anyone, as opposed to the believer who possesses wealth of which he spends both secretly and publicly. The first interpretation which Shaykh al-Islâm mentioned is more likely.

incapable of anything, and another whom Allah had provided with excellent provisions that he spends from secretly and publicly. He ﷻ struck that [second individual] as an example of Himself, for He ﷻ is knowing, just, capable, enjoins justice, and upholds equity upon a straight path, as the Most High said,

$$شَهِدَ اللَّهُ أَنَّهُ لَا إِلَهَ إِلَّا هُوَ وَالْمَلَائِكَةُ وَأُولُو الْعِلْمِ قَائِمًا بِالْقِسْطِ لَا إِلَهَ إِلَّا هُوَ الْعَزِيزُ الْحَكِيمُ$$

Allah witnesses that there is no deity except Him, and [so do] the angels and those of knowledge - [that He is] maintaining [creation] in justice. There is no deity except Him, the Exalted in Might, the Wise. ['Âli 'Imrân (3): 18]

… and Hood ﷺ said,

$$إِنَّ رَبِّي عَلَى صِرَاطٍ مُسْتَقِيمٍ$$

Indeed, my Lord is upon a straight path.[1] [Hood (11): 56]

---

[1] The idol-worshipper is burdened with protecting, defending, and supporting his object of worship – like the polytheists from the people of Ibrâheem ﷺ who said upon seeing their gods crushed, **"They said [to each other], 'Indeed, you are the wrongdoers.'"** [al-Anbiyâ' (21): 64] They called one another wrongdoers because they left their gods unguarded. Likewise with everyone who worships other than Allah; he needs to guard, protect, and support his object of worship, for his object of worship is incompetent and needy. Hence, it is a burden on whoever is devout to it and chooses to worship it, and hence the worshipper of other than Allah is miserable in this world and the hereafter. As for Allah ﷻ, He is capable, knowledgeable, wise, and just, as the Most High said, **"Allah witnesses that there is no deity except Him, and [so do] the angels and those of knowledge - [that He is] maintaining [creation] in justice."** [Âl-'Imrân (3): 18] Elsewhere, He also said, **"Indeed, my Lord is upon a straight path."** [Hood (11): 56] Therefore, He ﷻ maintains justice upon a straight path; all His actions are upon a straight path, for all His actions are wise and justice, and His commands as well are all wise and just. His actions and commands are exactly like His names and His self, in their beauty and perfection.

Does this slave who is incapable of generosity equate with this [individual] who is capable of generosity, and is generous to the people secretly and publicly? Likewise, He ﷻ is capable of being generous to His slaves, and is constantly practicing generosity with them. How then can the incompetent slave that is incapable of anything be resembled to Him ﷻ by being considered His partner [in worship]? This is like the one whom Allah granted wealth from which he spends by night and day.

In the second example, imagine two individuals, one of which is mute; he does not comprehend, nor does he speak, nor is he capable of anything. In addition to that, he is a burden on his master; wherever he directs him, he never brings about any good. So, he serves no benefit whatsoever, rather he is a burden on his caretaker. The other is knowledgeable, just, enjoins justice, practices justice, and so he is upon a straight path. This is like the one whom Allah granted wisdom upon which he acts and teaches to others.

For this reason, the people used to exalt the family of al-'Abbâs. 'Abdullâh used to teach the people, and his brother used to feed the people, and they were highly revered for that. Similarly, when Mu'âwiya saw the people asking Ibn 'Umar about the *manâsik* (rites of Hajj) and him giving them *fatâwâ* (edicts), he said, "This, by Allah, is nobility," or something to that effect.

'Umar b. al-Khattâb ﷺ competed with Abu Bakr ﷺ in charity, as was confirmed in *as-Saheeh*, on the authority of 'Umar b. al-Khattâb ﷺ, who said, "The Messenger of Allah ﷺ commanded us to give in charity, and that coincided with [a surplus in] my wealth, so I said, 'If there is ever a day when I will outrace Abu Bakr, today is the day I will outrace him.' I came forward with half of my wealth, so the Messenger of Allah ﷺ said to me, **'What have you kept for your family?'** I said, 'Its equivalent.' Abu Bakr came forward with all of his wealth, so the Messenger of Allah ﷺ said to him, **'What have you kept for your family?'** He said, 'I kept for them Allah and His Messenger.' So, I said: 'Never will I race you towards anything again.'"[1] What 'Umar did was the permissible *munâfasa* and *ghibta*, but the condition

---

[1] Narrated by Abu Dâwud (1678), at-Tirmidhi (3939), and was deemed *hasan* by al-Albâni.

of aṣ-Ṣiddeeq 🖼️ was superior to his; he was completely void of any competition, and would not look to the condition of anyone else.

Similar to this was Moosâ 🖼️ in the hadith of *al-Mi'râj* (the ascension); he displayed *munâfasa* and *ghibṭa* of the Prophet 🖼️ to the degree that he cried when the Prophet 🖼️ proceeded past him. It was said to him, **"What makes you cry?"** He said, **"I cry because of a young man that was sent after me; more people enter Paradise from his nation than those entering from my nation."**[1] This was collected in *aṣ-Ṣaḥeeḥayn*. According to another wording, though inauthentic, that has been narrated, "We passed by a man that was raising his voice [saying], 'You honored him and preferred him!' We were raised to him, so we gave him [the greeting of] *as-Salâm*, and he returned the [greeting of] *as-Salâm*. Then, he said: 'Who is this with you, O Jibreel?' He said, 'This is Ahmad.' He said, 'Welcome is the unlettered Prophet who conveyed the message of his Lord and sincerely advised his nation.' Then, we proceeded onward, so I said: 'O Jibreel, who was that?' He said, 'this was Moosâ b. 'Imrân.' I said, 'And who was he reproaching?' He said, 'He was reproaching his Lord about you.' I said, 'He raises his voice to his Lord?!' He said, 'Verily, Allah has known his truthfulness.'"[2]

'Umar b. al-Khaṭṭâb was resembled to Moosâ 🖼️, and the condition of our Prophet 🖼️ was better than the condition of Moosâ, for he possessed none of this whatsoever. Likewise, among the companions were Abu 'Ubayda b. al-Jarrâḥ 🖼️ and his likes who were secure of all these matters. They were superior a degree from those possessing *munâfasa* and *ghibṭa*, even though these were permissible[3]. For this reason, Abu 'Ubayda deserved being

---

[1] Narrated by al-Bukhâri (3887) and Muslim (163).

[2] With the wording: "his sharpness," instead of "his truthfulness," this has been collected by Ibn 'Arfa in his famous treatise. Ibn Katheer said: "Its chain is *ghareeb*." Al-Albâni said in *al-Isrâ' wal-Mi'râj*: "Its chain has two defects."

[3] Mentioning Abu 'Ubayda here, after the mention of 'Umar 🖼️, is because the Prophet 🖼️ once said, **"I will send with you a man that is trustworthy; truly trustworthy."** The people all became hopeful, and 'Umar as well hoped to be that man. His wishing for leadership on that day wasn't out of love for prominence and leadership, but out of competitiveness in good. As for Abu 'Ubayda, he did not carry that hopefulness nor that competitiveness, and thus Abu 'Ubayda 🖼️ was most deserving to be that man, since his inner-self didn't contend for it – as opposed to 'Umar. Even though 'Umar is undoubtedly superior to Abu 'Ubayda, this competitiveness is still a lesser degree, and the higher degree is to love good and seek it without looking at the actions of others or

Ameen al-Umma (the trustee of the nation), because when the trustee does not covet what he has been entrusted with, he is more deserving of being entrusted than someone whose coveting is feared. Due to this, the castrated are trusted with regards to the women and youth, and the lesser governance can be entrusted to those known to not covet the greater, and wealth can be entrusted to those known to be without tendency to take from it. Were someone entrusted whose soul harbors treachery, this is resembled to a wolf that is entrusted with sheep; he is incapable of upholding this trust because of the desire within him for that which he has been entrusted.

In the hadith narrated by Imâm Aḥmad in his *Musnad*, on the authority of Anas ﷺ, it states, "As we were sitting with the Messenger of Allah ﷺ one day, he said, **'Now, a man from the people of Paradise will emerge before you from this pathway.'** A man from the Anṣâr emerged, one whose beard was dripping from his ablution water, and whose sandals were hung in his left hand, and he gave the [greeting of] *as-Salâm*. On the following day, the Prophet ﷺ said its likes, and that [same] man emerged in equal fashion. When the Prophet ﷺ stood [and left], 'Abdullâh b. 'Amr b. al-'Âṣ followed him and said, 'I disputed with my father, and swore to not enter upon him for three [days]. Would you accept hosting me until the three have passed?' He said, 'Yes.' Thereafter, 'Abdullâh used to inform that he slept there with him for three nights, but did not see him stand [in prayer] at night whatsoever, and would only overturn on his bed, mention Allah, and make *takbeer* upon awakening, and would do this until the *fajr* prayer. However, I would not hear him say anything but good. When the three nights concluded, and I was on the verge of belittling his actions, I said, 'O slave of Allah, there was no anger or abandonment between me and my father, but I heard the Messenger of Allah ﷺ say thrice, **'A man from the people of**

competing with them. Likewise with Moosâ ﷺ; he also had a shade of competitiveness and jealous admiration, even though he was the most complete human being after our Prophet ﷺ and after Ibrâheem ﷺ. Hence, Ibn Taymiya mentioning Moosâ ﷺ and 'Umar ﷺ here was to prove that competing in good is permissible, even though the more perfect state is that of those in whom this doesn't exist. Of course, being superior and more perfect in this particular facet does not necessitate being better and more superior from every angle, or in totality – for 'Umar is superior to Abu 'Ubayda by *ijmâ'* (unanimity). This superiority is solely regarding the issue of leadership and trustworthiness, in light of the inner-self not being inclined to competition.

Paradise will emerge before you,' and it was you that emerged in the three times. Thus, I sought housing with you to observe your actions and emulate them. Yet, I did not see that you do much, so what brought you to that [status] which the Messenger of Allah ﷺ stated?' He said, 'It is nothing different than what you saw, except that I do not harbor within me any deceit or envy against a Muslim for the good that Allah granted him.' 'Abdullâh said, 'This is what brought you there, and this is what we cannot bear.'"[1] Hence, the statement of 'Abdullâh b. 'Amr to him, 'This is what brought you there, and this is what we cannot bear,' alludes to him being clear and free of all the types of *hasad*.

With this [virtue], Allah ﷺ praised the Ansâr, and said,

وَلَا يَجِدُونَ فِي صُدُورِهِمْ حَاجَةً مِّمَّا أُوتُوا وَيُؤْثِرُونَ عَلَى أَنفُسِهِمْ وَلَوْ كَانَ بِهِمْ خَصَاصَةٌ

And they find not any want in their chests of what they were given, but give [them] preference over themselves, even though they are in privation. [al-Hashr (59): 9]

…meaning: of what their brothers from among the *Muhâjireen* have been given. Some *tafsir* scholars said that, **"And they find not any want in their chests,"** [al-Hashr (59): 9] means, 'Envy or rage from what the *Muhâjireen* have been given.' Then, some said, '…from the money of the spoils,' while others said, '…from virtue and precedence.' Therefore, they do not find within themselves any want of what they have been given of wealth and reputation, and envy occurs regarding these.

As well, there existed *munâfasa* in the religion between al-Aws and al-Khazraj. Whenever they would perform what earned them preference in the sight of Allah and His Messenger, the other loved that they perform its likes. This is being competitive in what nears them to Allah ﷺ, as He said, **"The last of it is musk. So for this let the competitors compete."** [al-Mutaffifeen (83): 26]

---

[1] Narrated by Ahmad (12633), and its verifier said: "Its chain is authentic."

X – The Condemned Envy

As for the entirely dispraised *ḥasad*, the Most High has said regarding the Jews,

$$وَدَّ كَثِيرٌ مِنْ أَهْلِ الْكِتَابِ لَوْ يَرُدُّونَكُم مِّن بَعْدِ إِيمَانِكُمْ كُفَّارًا حَسَدًا مِّنْ عِندِ أَنفُسِهِم مِّن بَعْدِ مَا تَبَيَّنَ لَهُمُ الْحَقُّ$$

Many of the People of the Scripture love that they could turn you back to disbelief after you have believed, out of envy from themselves [even] after the truth has become clear to them. [al-Baqara (2): 109]

The words **"they love"** mean they wish for your apostasy because of envy. Hence, it was the envy that generated this love after the truth had become clear to them. This [envy] was because upon them noticing that you have acquired such a blessing, a blessing that they themselves did not acquire, they envied you. Likewise in the other verse,

$$أَمْ يَحْسُدُونَ النَّاسَ عَلَىٰ مَا آتَاهُمُ اللَّهُ مِن فَضْلِهِ فَقَدْ آتَيْنَا آلَ إِبْرَاهِيمَ الْكِتَابَ وَالْحِكْمَةَ وَآتَيْنَاهُم مُّلْكًا عَظِيمًا ۞ فَمِنْهُم مَّنْ آمَنَ بِهِ وَمِنْهُم مَّن صَدَّ عَنْهُ ۚ وَكَفَىٰ بِجَهَنَّمَ سَعِيرًا$$

Or do they envy people for what Allah has given them of His bounty? But We had already given the family of Abraham the Scripture and wisdom and conferred upon them a great kingdom. And some among them believed in it, and some among them were averse to it. And sufficient is Hell as a blaze. [an-Nisâ' (4): 54-55]

As well, the Most High said,

$$\text{قُلْ أَعُوذُ بِرَبِّ الْفَلَقِ ۞ مِن شَرِّ مَا خَلَقَ ۞ وَمِن شَرِّ غَاسِقٍ إِذَا وَقَبَ ۞ وَمِن}$$

$$\text{شَرِّ النَّفَّاثَاتِ فِي الْعُقَدِ ۞ وَمِن شَرِّ حَاسِدٍ إِذَا حَسَدَ}$$

Say: "I seek refuge in the Lord of daybreak. From the evil of that which He created. And from the evil of darkness when it settles. And from the evil of the blowers in knots. And from the evil of an envier when he envies." [Surat al-Falaq]

A group of *tafsir* scholars mentioned that this [*surah*] descended because of the Jews envying the Prophet ﷺ until they had Labeed b. al-A'ṣam, the Jew, employ witchcraft against him[1].

Therefore, the envier who hates the blessing that Allah blessed [another] with is an oppressor and transgressor, and the hater of inferiority who loves to match him is prohibited except in matters that bring one closer to Allah[2]. So if he loves to spend the likes of what he spent, which brings him closer to Allah, there is no harm in this, though his heart ignoring this whereby he does not look to the condition of others is even better.

Now, if the bearer of this envy acts upon it, then he is a transgressing oppressor that deserves punishment unless he repents[3], and the envied is a victim of oppression that is

---

[1] See: al-Bukhâri (5766, 5863, 2189) and Muslim (2189).

[2] Hating what Allah ﷻ favored His slaves with is always unlawful. As for hating that a person be superior to him – when this is regarding worldly matters, this is generally prohibited. But when this is regarding a matter of religiosity, this is permissible, although the most perfect state is not harboring that inside oneself. And the basis of envy in religious matters is with regards to beneficial knowledge, and the wealth that is spent in the way of Allah.

[3] The action for which its doer is punishable could be the action of the heart itself, and could combine the actions of the limbs as well. The person who hates the blessings of Allah ﷻ upon one of His creatures, and wishes he would be stripped of this blessing, is an oppressor that has wronged the envied person. Furthermore, Allah ﷻ could decree that this blessing be removed from the envied person because of such envy, just as Allah ﷻ sometimes decrees things because of sorcery. Envy and sorcery are of the unlawful means which have an effect by the decree of Allah ﷻ, even though their practitioner is sinful and punishable for his actions. As for the envied, he is a victim of oppression that is commanded to be patient with what afflicted him. This is the intended meaning behind our statement that envy is true; it is a true reality that exists. By truth, we do not

commanded with patience and *taqwâ* (piety). He should patiently endure the harm of the envier, and pardon and dismiss him, as the Most High said,

$$وَدَّ كَثِيرٌ مِنْ أَهْلِ الْكِتَابِ لَوْ يَرُدُّونَكُم مِّن بَعْدِ إِيمَانِكُمْ كُفَّارًا حَسَدًا مِّنْ عِندِ أَنفُسِهِم مِّن بَعْدِ مَا تَبَيَّنَ لَهُمُ الْحَقُّ فَاعْفُوا وَاصْفَحُوا حَتَّى يَأْتِيَ اللَّهُ بِأَمْرِهِ$$

Many of the People of the Scripture love that they could turn you back to disbelief after you have believed, out of envy from themselves [even] after the truth has become clear to them. So pardon and overlook until Allah delivers His command. [al-Baqara (2): 109]

Yoosuf ﷺ was afflicted with the envy of his brothers, wherein they said,

$$إِذْ قَالُوا لَيُوسُفُ وَأَخُوهُ أَحَبُّ إِلَى أَبِينَا مِنَّا وَنَحْنُ عُصْبَةٌ إِنَّ أَبَانَا لَفِي ضَلَالٍ مُّبِينٍ$$

Yoosuf and his brother are more beloved to our father than we, while we are a clan. Indeed, our father is in clear error. [Yoosuf (12): 8]

They envied the two due to their father preferring them, and thus Ya'qoob said to Yoosuf,

---

mean that to say that it is correct and fair. Likewise, the statement of the Prophet ﷺ, **"The [evil] eye is true,"** [Narrated by Muslim (2188)] means that it truly exists and has an effect. The evil eye is more specific than envy, for it isn't contingent upon hating the blessing or wishing that it be removed from others. In fact, he could afflict himself or others with that [evil] eye, for this eye happens when a person sees a blessing that he admires, but does not attribute it to Allah ﷻ, and does not say, *"Mâ Shâ Allâh,"* or the likes. It has an effect, by the decree of Allah, just as envy has an effect by the decree of Allah. Allah ﷻ has commanded His slaves to seek refuge **"from the evil of an envier when he envies,"** [al-Falaq (113): 5] and that indicates that envy indeed has an effect. Finally, this internal envy – which is an action of the heart – is usually paired with the actions of the limbs, and thus most enmities between people are resultant of envy; may Allah save us from it.

$$\text{لَا تَقْصُصْ رُؤْيَاكَ عَلَىٰ إِخْوَتِكَ فَيَكِيدُوا لَكَ كَيْدًا إِنَّ الشَّيْطَانَ لِلْإِنسَانِ عَدُوٌّ مُّبِينٌ}$$

Do not relate your vision to your brothers or they will contrive against you a plan. Indeed Satan, to man, is a manifest enemy. [Yoosuf (12): 5]

Then, they oppressed him by discussing his murder, by casting him into the well, and by selling him as a slave to those going to the lands of disbelief, which in turn made him the slave of a disbelieving people.

Furthermore, Yoosuf was afflicted – after being oppressed – with someone who invites him to fornicating, and seduces him towards it. She even sought the help of those that could aid her, but he remained chaste, chose prison over fornication, and preferred the worldly punishment over the anger of Allah. Hence, he was a victim of [further] oppression at the hands of someone who desired him for wicked aims. This lover loved him for her own selfish desires, and it would have resulted in her misery and his if had he complied with her demands, and these haters harbored hatred for him that resulted in him being cast into the well, and then thrown into slavery, against his will. So, these [brothers] removed him from complete freedom to unjust servitude against his will, while she drove him to choose being a jailed prisoner by choice. Thus, this was a greater tribulation for him, and his patience here was a willing patience that was paired with *taqwa*. As for his patience in the face of their oppression, that was an example of enduring calamities; those who do not endure them with dignified patience are [eventually] soothed just like the animals. The second patience was the more superior of the two, and thus He said,

$$\text{إِنَّهُ مَن يَتَّقِ وَيَصْبِرْ فَإِنَّ اللَّهَ لَا يُضِيعُ أَجْرَ الْمُحْسِنِينَ}$$

Indeed, he who exhibits *taqwa* (i.e., fears Allah) and is patient, then indeed, Allah does not allow to be lost the reward of those who do good.[1] [Yoosuf (12): 90]

The same applies to every believer who is harmed for his belief; when he is pushed to disbelief, sin, or disobedience, and he is harmed or punished if he does not comply, but chooses the harm and punishment over parting with his religion – whether that [harm] be imprisonment or expulsion from his land. This is like what happened to the *Muhâjireen* who were tortured and harmed, and chose leaving their homelands over leaving their religion.

The Prophet 🕊 was subjected to many types of harm, and used to exhibit this voluntary patience, for he was only harmed in order that he discontinue these actions which he practiced by choice. This was even greater than the patience of Yoosuf 🕊, because Yoosuf was only pushed to fornication, and was only punished with imprisonment when he did not comply. The Prophet 🕊 and his Companions were pushed to disbelieve, and their punishment for not complying was murder, and other lesser harms, the least of which was imprisonment. The polytheists had imprisoned him and Banu Hâshim in a valley for some time. Later, when Abu Ṭâlib died, they intensified their efforts against him 🕊. Then, when the *Anṣâr* pledged allegiance and they learned of that, they began trying to impede his exit [from Mecca], and tried stopping him and his companions from doing that. None used to migrate except secretly, aside from 'Umar b. al-Khaṭṭâb 🕊 and his likes. In this manner, they drove them to abandon their homes, alongside preventing and imprisoning some of them from doing so[2].

---

[1] Allah 🕊 makes the outcome of patience entirely good, especially the voluntary patience, even though the outcome of being patience with calamities is good as well. When Yoosuf 🕊 was patient with what his brothers did, Allah 🕊 rewarded him by making him honored with al-'Azeez, and then supported him against those who wronged him.

[2] And the outcome which Allah 🕊 granted His Messenger 🕊 and his Companions was entirely good, after the patience they exhibited in Mecca. Allah 🕊 established the believers through migrating to Madinah, and had them return to Mecca eight years later after becoming mighty and empowered. As well, Allah 🕊 granted them conquest of the Arabian Peninsula, and all the surrounding lands, until they became the kings of the earth after once not finding any food but the leaves of trees; may Allah be pleased with them.

The harms and calamites that the believers encountered [here] were by their choosing, out of obedience to Allah and His Messenger. It was not like the heavenly [destined] calamities that occur without the slave's choice, like the separation between Yoosuf and his father, but rather [it was] like the imprisonment of Yoosuf. This is the nobler of the two types, and its possessors are greater in rank. Although the sufferer of calamities is [still] rewarded for his patience and contentment, and his sins are expiated by his calamities, the other who suffers voluntarily, out of obedience to Allah and His Messenger, is rewarded for these calamities themselves and they are written for him as good deeds. The Most High said,

ذٰلِكَ بِأَنَّهُمْ لَا يُصِيبُهُمْ ظَمَأٌ وَلَا نَصَبٌ وَلَا مَخْمَصَةٌ فِي سَبِيلِ اللَّهِ وَلَا يَطَئُونَ مَوْطِئًا يَغِيظُ الْكُفَّارَ وَلَا يَنَالُونَ مِنْ عَدُوٍّ نَيْلًا إِلَّا كُتِبَ لَهُم بِهِ عَمَلٌ صَالِحٌ إِنَّ اللَّهَ لَا يُضِيعُ أَجْرَ الْمُحْسِنِينَ

That is because they are not afflicted by thirst or fatigue or hunger in the cause of Allah, nor do they tread on any ground that enrages the disbelievers, nor do they inflict upon an enemy any infliction but that is registered for them as a righteous deed. Indeed, Allah does not allow to be lost the reward of the doers of good. [at-Tawbah (9): 120]

This differs from the calamities that befall a slave without his choice, such as sickness, the death of someone dear to him, or thieves taking his wealth. With these, reward is only granted for being patient through them, not for the actual calamity itself. However, the calamity does expiate sins, while the reward is only for voluntary actions and what generates from them.

So those who are harmed for their *eemân*, out of obedience to Allah and His Messenger, and as a result experience harm, or sickness, or imprisonment, or separation from their lands, or loss of wealth or family, or beating, or insult, or decreased authority or wealth –

they are, in that regard, upon the path of the prophets and their followers, just like the *Muhâjireen*. Such are rewarded for the harm they incur, and it is written for them as good deeds, just as the combatant is rewarded for what he experiences of hunger, thirst, exhaustion, and infuriation of the disbelievers. Even though these events are not actions he performed, they were caused by his voluntary action, and these are what are meant by "generated" acts.

People have differed: are these to be considered acts performed by the doer of their cause, or by Allah, or do they have no doer? The correct view is that they are shared between the doer of the cause, and all the other causes, and thus they are written as good deeds for him.

The point being is that envy is one of the diseases of the heart, and an overwhelming disease that few people have escaped. For this reason, it is said, "No *jasad* (body) is void of *hasad*, except that the malicious displays it and the dignified conceals it." Similarly, it was said to al-Hasan al-Basri, "Does a believer envy?" He said, "How fast you forget the brothers of Yoosuf! But bury it in your chests, for it will not harm you so long as it does not cause your hand or tongue to transgress."[1]

---

[1] His statement, "Does a believer envy?" – refers to a person in whose heart is minimal *eemân*. The believer in whose heart is complete *eemân* does not partake in this unlawful envy, and thus there is no doubt that the brothers of Yoosuf ﷺ fell into this envy because of the deficiency of their *eemân*.

As for his statement, "But bury it in your chests," this means smother it within your chest until it leaves by the permission of Allah ﷻ once it has been resisted and fought off. Therefore, the believer is obligated to hate that about himself and repel it, and ponder over the blessings of Allah that he enjoys and His countless favors, and that it was Allah ﷻ who divided these provisions, just as the Prophet ﷺ said, **"Whoever says in his morning, '*Allâhumma Mâ Asbaha Bi Min Ni'matin Aw Bi-Ahadin Min Khalqik, Fa-Minka Wahdaka Lâ Shareeka Lak, Fa-Lakal Hamdu wa Lak ash-Shukr* (O Allah, I have no favor this morning, nor does anyone of Your creation, except [it's] from You alone, without any partners – so for You is all praise, and for you is all thanks),' – then he has given due thanks for his day. And whoever says this in the evening, then he has given due thanks for his night."** [Narrated by Abu Dâwud (5073) and Ibn Mâjah (858), was deemed weak by Shaykh al-Albâni, and was deemed *hasan* by Shaykh Ibn Bâz in *at-Tuhfa*] If a person were to reflect on this supplication, and were his heart to internalize it, the envy of his heart would certainly vanish, by the permission of Allah.

Whoever finds within himself envy against others, he is obligated to counter it with patience and *taqwâ*, whereby he hates that about himself[1].

Many people who have religiosity do not transgress against the person they envy, and hence they do not aid those who oppress him. However, they also do not fulfill their duty of upholding his rights. Were someone to criticize him, they would neither agree with him being criticized nor mention his merits. Likewise, were someone to compliment him, they would remain silent. Such people are liable for being neglectful of the commands pertaining to his rights, not for being transgressors against him[2]. Their repayment is that they will be cheated of their rights, will similarly not be supported in certain situations[3], and will not be supported against those who oppress them – just as they did not support this envied individual.

As for someone who transgressed with a statement or action, then such [a person] is punished[4], while whoever exhibits *taqwâ* and patience will not be included under the oppressors. Allah ﷻ will favor such people because of their *taqwâ*, like what happened to Zaynab b. Jaḥsh ﵂ [5]. She was the one who was comparable to 'Â'isha from among the

---

[1] He should hate about himself that he wishes the blessing would vanish, and hate about himself that he wishes none would ever be superior to him.

[2] The rights of a Muslim upon another Muslim are two types: a right of action and a right of abstention. He must perform the mandatory actions of goodness towards him, and must abstain from the unlawful actions that harm him. If he were to abstain from harming his brother, but did not defend him in his absence and did not mention his virtues and merits, then he has not transgressed against him, but still has not performed his duty towards his brother; namely defending his reputation in his absence and mentioning his merits. By failing to do so, he has not fulfilled his rights.

[3] In some instances, no one defends them and upholds justice regarding them – despite them being wronged and deserving of defense – because Allah ﷻ repaid them with His perfect justice, due to them previously neglecting the rights of their brothers.

[4] The words of Shaykh al-Islâm (may Allah bestow mercy upon him) do not necessitate that someone who neglects an obligation towards his brother is only punishable in this world. Rather, he could also be punished for this in the hereafter as well. For instance, if a person were to see someone killing another, and he was capable of defending him, but between him and this victim was some enmity and so left him to be killed, then he is undoubtedly sinful and deserving of punishment for that in the hereafter.

[5] When the incident of *al-Ifk* (the Scandal) took place, the Prophet ﷺ asked Zaynab ﵂ about 'Â'isha ﵂, and she said, "I protect my hearing and sight [from slander]." [Narrated by al-Bukhâri and Muslim]

wives of the Prophet ﷺ, and women envying one another is largely predominant, especially those married to one husband. A woman exhibits this protective jealousy over her husband because of her share of him, since she loses out on a portion of that share during polygyny. Due to this factor, envy commonly takes place between two people that share leadership or wealth; whenever one takes a portion of it, and [consequently] the other is deprived of it. It also exists between peers, due to their hatred that the other surpasses them. This is like the envy of Yoosuf's brothers, and like the envy that one of Âdam's sons harbored for his brother; he envied him because Allah accepted his sacrifice, and did not accept the other's sacrifice, so he envied him due to what Allah preferred him with of *eemân* and *taqwâ* – just like the Jews' envy of the Muslims[1] – and he killed him as a result of that. For this reason, it was said: "The first sins that Allah was disobeyed with were three: covetousness, arrogance, and envy; Âdam coveted, Iblees was arrogant, and Cane was envious when he killed Abel."[2] Also, in the hadith: "Three [qualities] no one escapes: envy, assumption, and [evil] omens – and I will inform you of what rescues from them; when you envy, do not loathe, and when you assume, do not investigate, and when you fear an omen, proceed onward." This was narrated by Ibn Abi ad-Dunyâ, on the authority of Abu Hurayra[3].

In *as-Sunan*, the Prophet ﷺ said, **"There has crawled towards you the disease of the nations before you – envy and hatred – and it is the shaver. I do not [intend to] say that which shaves hair, but rather it shaves the religion."[4]** Here, he named it a disease,

---

[1] As the Most High said, **"Many of the People of the Scripture love that they could turn you back to disbelief after you have believed, out of envy from themselves [even] after the truth has become clear to them."** [al-Baqara (2): 109] Hence, the Jews are the most envious people of the Muslims, and for that reason they are keen to spread [among them] corruption, sins, and disbelief; may Allah save us from that.
[2] Envy and pride are mutually inclusive, and thus Iblees was too proud to prostrate before Adam, and that was due to his envy of Âdam ﷺ.
[3] Al-'Ajlooni said in *Kashf al-Khafâ'* (2208): "Its chain is weak." Ibn al-Jawzi said in *Tadhkirat al-Mawdoo'ât*: "Two of its narrators were deemed weak." Al-'Irâqi said in *Takhreej al-Ihyâ'*: "It was collected by Ibn Abi ad-Dunyâ in his book *Dhamm al-Hasad*, on the authority of Abu Hurayrah, but it contains Ya'qoob ibn Muhammad az-Zuhri and Moosâ ibn Ya'qoob az-Zam'i who were both deemed weak by the majority. The second narration was also narrated by Ibn Abi ad-Dunyâ, through 'Abdur-Rahmân ibn Mu'âwiyah, and it is a weak *mursal* report."
[4] Narrated by at-Tirmidhi (2641) and deemed *hasan* by al-Albâni.

just as he named stinginess a disease in his statement, **"And what disease is more of an ailment than stinginess?"**[1] Through that, it has become known that it is a disease. In another hadith, it came, **"And I seek refuge with You from the evil *akhlâq* (manners), desires, and diseases,"**[2] wherein he ﷺ combined between [mentioning] diseases, desires, and *akhlâq*. *Akhlâq* are what the inner-self has become accustomed to – its habits. The Most High said,

$$\text{وَإِنَّكَ لَعَلَى خُلُقٍ عَظِيمٍ}$$

Indeed, you are upon a great *khuluq* (pl. *akhlâq*; moral character). [al-Qalam (68): 4]

Ibn 'Abbâs, Ibn 'Uyayna, and Ahmad b. Hanbal – may Allah be pleased with them – said, "Upon a great religion." In another wording, Ibn 'Abbâs said, "Upon the religion of Islam." Similarly, 'Â'isha ◈ said, "His *akhlâq* were the Qur'an."[3] Likewise, al-Hasan al-Basri said, "The manners of the Qur'an are the great *khuluq*." As for desires, they could be momentary, and diseases are sickness – that which corrupts and pains the heart.

In the first hadith, he ﷺ paired between envy and hatred because the envier first hates that Allah favors this other [individual], then it transforms into hating him. This is because hating what is being given to someone necessitates hating the one to whom it was given. Since he hates the blessing of Allah and wishes for its departure, and it will not depart without his departure, thus he hates him and wishes for his disappearance. Envy elicits transgression, as Allah ﷻ informed about those before us, that they differed after the knowledge came to them due to animosity between them. Their differing was not due to a lack of knowledge, for they knew the truth, but rather they transgressed against one another in the manner that an envier transgresses against the envied[4].

---

[1] Narrated by al-Bukhâri (3137).
[2] Narrated by at-Tirmidhi (3843) with the wording: **"O Allah, I seek refuge with You from the evil *akhlâq*, actions, and desires,"** and it was deemed authentic by al-Albâni.
[3] Narrated by Muslim (746).
[4] Therefore, the diseases of the nations were not always centered on ignorance. Rather, knowledge could be present, but does not benefit due to the existence of animosity along

In *as-Ṣaḥeeḥayn*, Anas b. Mâlik ﷺ narrated that the Prophet ﷺ said, **"Do not envy one another, do not hate one another, do not forsake one another, do not sever ties with one another, and be, the slaves of Allah, brothers. It is not lawful for a Muslim to abandon his brother for over three nights, wherein they meet and ignore one another, and the better of the two is the one who gives [the greeting]** *as-Salâm* **first."**[12] Also, he ﷺ said in the hadith that was also agreed upon and narrated by Anas, **"By the One in whose hand is my soul, none of you [truly] believes until he loves for his brother what he loves for himself."**[3]

The Most High has said,

---

with it. It was not the knowledge which generated the misguidance and disunity, but rather it was the animosity and oppression that elicited it.

[1] Narrated by al-Bukhâri (6065) and Muslim (2559).

[2] Hating one another, forsaking one another, and severing ties with one another has causes, just as love and affection have causes. Here, the prohibition of hating and forsaking one another includes the causes which lead to it, such as speaking to his brother in a manner that hurts him, or insults him, or mocks him, and the similar behaviors which evoke hating and forsaking one another. Thus, the Prophet ﷺ said, **"No two should have a private dialogue without the third, because that saddens him."** This was narrated by al-Bukhâri (6290) with the wording, **"When you are three, then no two men should have a private dialogue without the third, unless you have [become] a bunch of people, for that saddens him."** This was also narrated by Muslim (2184) with the wording, **"When you are three, then no two should have a private dialogue without the third, unless you have [become] a bunch of people, because that saddens him."** This was also narrated by Ibn Mâjah (3042) with the wording, **"When you are three, no two should have a private dialogue without their companion, unless you have [become] a bunch of people, for that saddens him."** This last wording was authenticated by al-Albâni. Therefore, every cause of saddening a Muslim is prohibited.

As for hating the sinners and disbelievers, that is obligatory – for that is hatred for [the sake of] Allah, not for selfish motives or desires, and he ﷺ has said, **"Love for Allah and hatred for Allah are the strongest handholds of** *eemân*.**"** [Narrated by al-Ḥâkim and aṭ-Ṭabarâni, and authenticated by al-Albâni in *Ṣaḥeeḥ al-Jâmi'* (2539) with the wording, **"The strongest handhold of** *eemân* **is loyalty for Allah and enmity for Allah, and loving for Allah and hating for Allah."**]

[3] Narrated by al-Bukhâri (13) and Muslim (45).

$$ \text{وَإِنَّ مِنكُمْ لَمَن لَيُبَطِّئَنَّ فَإِنْ أَصَابَتْكُم مُّصِيبَةٌ قَالَ قَدْ أَنْعَمَ اللَّهُ عَلَيَّ إِذْ لَمْ أَكُن مَّعَهُمْ} $$

$$ \text{شَهِيدًا ۝ وَلَئِنْ أَصَابَكُمْ فَضْلٌ مِّنَ اللَّهِ لَيَقُولَنَّ كَأَن لَّمْ تَكُن بَيْنَكُمْ وَبَيْنَهُ مَوَدَّةٌ يَا لَيْتَنِي} $$

$$ \text{كُنتُ مَعَهُمْ فَأَفُوزَ فَوْزًا عَظِيمًا} $$

And indeed, there is among you he who lingers behind; and if disaster strikes you, he says, "Allah has favored me in that I was not present with them." But if bounty comes to you from Allah, he will surely say, as if there had never been between you and him any affection, "Oh, I wish I had been with them so I could have attained a great attainment." [an-Nisâ' (4): 72-73]

These lingerers did not love for their believing brothers what they loved for themselves. In fact, if a disaster strikes them, they rejoice that it was particular to them[1], and if a bounty reaches them, they are not happy for them because of it[2]. Instead, they wish they could have a share of it. They do not rejoice for anything except attaining a worldly matter, or being excused from a worldly evil, since they do not love Allah, His Messenger, and the home of the Hereafter. Had they, they would have loved their brothers, loved what reached them of His bounty, and would have been pained by the calamities that struck them. Whoever is not delighted by what delights the believers, and bothered by what bothers the believers, then he is not from them.

---

[1] If the Muslims are afflicted with a calamity, he considers it a bounty and favor of Allah upon him that he was not present. Hence, he does not consider himself a part of these afflicted people, while the true believer is pained by the calamity even if he was not present himself. This is because he feels that he and the afflicted individuals are a single body.

[2] Had there been in his heart any love or affection for the believers, he would have rejoiced for their joy, but all that concerns him is that he was not present for this worldly bounty, and this grieves him. As for the true believers, you find them happy for one another. For example, when Allah ﷻ accepted the repentance of the three who lingered behind [the army], of whom was Ka'b ibn Mâlik ﵁, the Companions rushed to congratulate them about their repentance. They rejoiced about the repentance, even though they hadn't committed the sin themselves, but still they were happy for one another.

In *as-Saheehayn*, 'Âmir said, "I heard an-Nu'mân b. al-Basheer delivering a sermon, and saying, 'I heard the Messenger of Allah ﷺ say, '**The example of the believers in their mutual love, mercy, and compassion, is that of a single body; when one of its parts are hurt, the entire body reacts to it with fever and lack of sleep.**'"[1] Also in *as-Saheehayn*, Abu Moosâ al-Ash'ari narrated that the Messenger of Allah ﷺ said, "**The believer to the believer is like a building; its parts reinforce one another,**" and he interlaced between his fingers[2].

Coveting is also a disease, and stinginess is also a disease. Envy is worse than stinginess, as per the hadith that was narrated by Abu Dâwud, that the Prophet ﷺ said, "**Envy devours good deeds just as fire consumes dry wood**[3], **and charity extinguishes sin just as water extinguishes fire.**"[4] That is because the stingy person deprives himself; while the envier hates that the slaves of Allah are blessed by Him. Also, a man could sometimes have generosity for those who help him attain his aims, while harboring envy for his peers. As well, he could have stinginess without envying others, and [all] that sprouts from coveting[5].

Allah, the Most High, said,

$$وَمَن يُوقَ شُحَّ نَفْسِهِ فَأُولَٰئِكَ هُمُ الْمُفْلِحُونَ$$

And whoever is protected from the coveting of his soul – it is those who will be the successful. [al-Ḥashr (59): 9]

---

[1] Narrated by al-Bukhâri (6011) and Muslim (2586).
[2] Narrated by al-Bukhâri (2446) and Muslim (2585).
[3] Narrated by Abu Dâwud (4903) and deemed weak by al-Albâni.
[4] Narrated by Ibn Mâjah (3973) and deemed authentic by al-Albâni.
[5] Coveting is the basis of stinginess and envy. Coveting is being keen to have what the people possess, and being interested in having it instead of them. As for the unlawful [coveting], this is when it deters from an obligation, such as impeding the payment of the mandatory *zakâh*, or the obligatory spending on the family and children, or upholding the mandatory right of the guest, and the likes. As for the disliked [coveting], this is by being strict with those he looks after, and limiting them to the mandatory amount and nothing more, in a manner that opposes the customary norms and honorable treatment.

In *as-Ṣaḥeeḥayn*, it was reported that the Prophet 🙼 said, **"Beware of coveting, for it destroyed those before you. It commanded them with stinginess, so they were stingy, and it commanded them with injustice, so they were unjust, and it commanded them with severing ties, so they severed ties."**[1] ʿAbdur-Raḥmân b. ʿAwf 🙼 would frequently supplicate during *ṭawâf* (circling the *Kaʿba*) by saying, "O Allah, shield me from the coveting of my inner-self." In turn, a man said to him, "How frequently you supplicate with this!" He responded, "If I am shielded from the coveting of my inner-self, I am shielded from coveting, committing injustice, and severing ties."[2] And envy is a form of injustice.

So stinginess and envy are diseases that cause the inner-self to hate what benefits it, and even love what harms it, and thus envy commonly coexists with contempt and anger.

XI – The Disease of *ʿIshq*

As for the disease of *shahwa* and *ʿishq* (excessive carnal love), this involves the inner-self loving what harms it, and could involve hating what benefits it[3]. *ʿIshq* is a spiritual disease, and when its effects on the body strengthen, it becomes a physical disease; either a mental disease like Melancholia[4] – and thus it's defined as: an obsessive disorder resembling Melancholia – or a bodily disease like weakness, malnutrition, and the likes.

---

[1] Narrated by Muslim, under the chapter: *The Prohibition of Injustice*, with the wording: **"Beware of coveting, for coveting destroyed those before you. It drove them to spill the blood of one another and usurp their properties."** I did not find it in al-Bukhâri.
[2] In another narration, "If I am shielded from the coveting of my inner-self, I will not steal, nor fornicate, nor do [anything sinful]." This is from the [deep] understanding of the Companions 🙼 regarding the disease of coveting, and that it is not limited to the wealth. Rather, it is to long for what people have at large. For instance, the one who fornicates only fornicates out of longing for what others have. Likewise, the one who looks at women is doing nothing but yearning for what is unlawful for him. This all goes back to coveting, which is the essence of every sin. The difference between coveting and stinginess is that stinginess is when a person withholds what he already possesses, which could be unlawful and could be disliked.
[3] Such as a person hating his wife because of his mistress.
[4] A mental condition characterized by severe depression, withdrawal, and delirium.

The intent here, though, is the disease of the heart – for it is the root cause behind the inner-self loving what harms it. It is just like an individual with bodily sickness who desires [to eat] what harms him; if he does not eat it, he is pained - and if he eats it, the disease within him increases and strengthens. Likewise, the *'âshiq* is harmed by being in contact with his objects of *'ishq,* via seeing, touching, and hearing them. In fact, he is [even] harmed by thinking about them, and imagining them, while longing for them. If he is prevented from his desire, he is pained and tortured, and if he is given what he desires, his disease increases and that becomes a reason for the pain to increase.

It has come in the hadith, **"Indeed, Allah protects His believing slave from this world just as one of you protects his sick from food and drink."**[1] As well, in the dialogue of Moosâ ﷺ, which was reported by Imâm Ahmad in his book *az-Zuhd,* on the authority of Wahb, Allah ﷻ says, "Verily, I shield My nearest slaves from the enjoyment of this world and its luxury, just as the compassionate shepherd shields his camels from what risks [their] death. Verily, I curb him from its stability and comfort just as the compassionate shepherd curbs his camels from resting in places of ambush. And that is not because of his unimportance to Me, but rather to fully and securely attain My honoring without being wounded by this world or smothered by [his] desires."[2] The cure for those diseased [with

---

[1] Narrated by Imâm Ahmad and al-Hâkim, and was deemed authentic by al-Albâni in *Saheeh al-Jâmi'* (1814) with the wording: **"Indeed, Allah – the Most High – protects His believing slave from this world, while He loves him, just as you protect your sick from food and drink, out of fear for him."**

[2] Although this report is from the narrations of Banu Isrâ'eel, its meaning is correct, for this concept is established by the Qur'an and the Sunnah. It is good when Allah ﷻ makes the believer's provision just enough, while making him content and pleased with that, for this world is insignificant to Allah ﷻ and thus He does not fully grant it to His nearest slaves. And whoever of them is given it, He guides them to spend it in goodness. However, the ideal state is that of those whose worldly provisions are just enough, and this concept is noticed in his words ﷺ, **"There is no troop that participates in battle and survives or gains spoils except that they have hastened two-thirds of their reward. And there is no troop that is afflicted or [returns] empty-handed except that their full reward is stowed for them."** [Narrated by Muslim (1906) with the wording, **"There is no troop or battalion that participates in battle and is granted safety and spoils except that they have hastened two-thirds of their rewards. And there is no troop or battle that is wounded or [returns] empty-handed except that**

'*ishq*] is by the removal of this sickness; namely by removing the condemned love from his heart.

People have two views with regards to '*ishq*. Some said it falls under will-powers, and that is the popular view. Others said it falls under perceptions[1], whereby it is a corruption in perception that causes the objects of '*ishq* to be seen as other than they actually are. They said: "For this reason, Allah cannot be described with '*ishq*, nor that He practices '*ishq*, for He is glorified above that, and because someone whose perceptions are flawed is not praiseworthy."[2]

As for the first group, some of them said, "He 🕮 can be described with '*ishq*, for it denotes complete love, and Allah loves and is loved." Additionally, it was reported that 'Abdil-Wâhid b. Zayd said, 'My slave continues drawing nearer to me, wherein he carries '*ishq* for Me and I carry '*ishq* for him.'[3]" This is the view of some Sufis.

The majority do not use this term in reference to Allah, because '*ishq* is excessive love which ventures beyond what is befitting, and loving Allah 🕮 has no end; there is no limit beyond which one should not venture.

They [also] said, "And '*ishq* is entirely dispraised. It is not praiseworthy in reference to loving the Creator, or the creation, because it is excessive love, which ventures beyond the praiseworthy limits. Also, the term '*ishq* is customarily used only with regards to a person loving a woman or child, and is not used for loving the likes of family, wealth, homeland, reputation, or the prophets and the righteous. Most of the time, it is paired with unlawful

---

their rewards are attained in full." In another narration by Muslim, **"and if they don't acquire any spoils, their reward is complete for them."**

[1] The correct position is that '*ishq* combines between corruption of perception and corruption of will-power. For this reason, it is possible that a person imagines a woman is beautiful while in reality the matter is not so; that is with regards to perceptions. Then, he could love and pursue her, and that is with regards to will-power.

[2] The majority of Ahl as-Sunnah do not permit using the term '*ishq* to describe Allah 🕮 , and Shaykh al-Islâm will discuss that matter shortly.

[3] Such words have not been confirmed about anyone from the *salaf* (early Muslims); none of them ever described Allah 🕮 as One who exhibits '*ishq*, or that '*ishq* is exhibited towards Him.

acts, such as loving a foreign woman or child, and the adjacent acts like the unlawful gaze, the unlawful touch, and other unlawful practices."

As for a man loving his wife or slave-girl to the degree that it removes him from being just, whereby he performs the unlawful and abandons the obligatory because of her, this is frequently the case. He [at times] oppresses his son from the old wife, due to his love for the new [wife], and obliges to her evil requests that harm his religiosity and worldly life. For instance, like allotting her inheritance she does not deserve, or giving her family loyalty and wealth that transgresses the limits of Allah, or spending on her extravagantly, or enabling her to practice forbidden matters that harm his religiosity and worldly life. All this pertains to the *'ishq* of those with whom intimacy is allowed.

What then is the case with having *'ishq* for a foreign women, or for the men of the world? That contains such corruption that none can encompass but the Lord of the slaves, and it is of the diseases that ruins a person's religion and honor, and may even ruin his mind and then his body. The Most High said,

$$\text{فَلَا تَخْضَعْنَ بِالْقَوْلِ فَيَطْمَعَ الَّذِي فِي قَلْبِهِ مَرَضٌ}$$

So do not be soft in speech, lest he in whose heart is a disease becomes hopeful. [al-Aḥzâb (33): 32]

Whenever the desired [individual] becomes soft, the diseased at heart who desires that image becomes hopeful[1]. This hope is what strengthens the will-power and pursuit, and in turn strengthens the disease. In contrast, if he despairs from pursuing, that despair terminates his hopes and in turn weakens the will-power, and subsequently weakens the [unlawful] love – for a person has no interest in pursuing that which he is hopeless of. Through that, the desire does not manifest into any actions whatsoever, aside from the

---

[1] Nowadays, people all over the world are viciously driven towards this disease. Western civilization is based on spreading immorality, provoking lusts, the desire of wealth, competing in that, and spreading malice, envy, stinginess, pride, and the likes. And many a times, wealth and leadership are centered around the unlawful sexual desires.

whispers of the inner-self, unless they are paired with words, glances, or the likes – in which case they would incur sin[1].

As for someone being afflicted with *'ishq*, but he remains chaste and is patient, he is rewarded for his fear of Allah[2]. It has been narrated in a hadith that, **"Whoever has *'ishq* but remains chaste, and conceals and is patient until he dies, then he is a martyr."**[3] This is known via the narration of Yaḥyâ al-Qattât, on the authority of Mujâhid, on the authority of Ibn 'Abbâs, as a *marfoo'* report, though it is questionable and unqualified to be used as evidence.

However, it is known from the evidences of the Sharia that when someone withholds from partaking in the unlawful, whether the glances, statements, or actions, and abstains from speaking about it so to not fall into unlawful speech, whether complaining to the creation or admitting immorality or somehow pursuing their beloved, and is patient upon the obedience of Allah, upon refraining from disobeying Him, and upon the pain of the *'ishq* in his heart – just as the afflicted is patient with his affliction – then such a person falls under those who exhibited *taqwâ* and patience, **"Indeed, he who exhibits *taqwa* (i.e., fears Allah) and is patient, then indeed, Allah does not allow to be lost the reward of those who do good."** [Yoosuf (12): 90]

This applies to the disease of envy, and every other disease of the inner-self. When the inner-self demands that which Allah hates, but one forbids it because of his fear of Allah, then he is included under His words,

---

[1] Therefore, in order for *'ishq* to exist in the heart, it must first be preceded by being hopeful for the object which he is infatuated with. Once that hope for it is severed, nothing regarding it will remain at that point but the whispers of the inner-self; no determination or resolve will remain within him towards that objective. And as for the whispers of the inner-self, so long as they aren't coupled with resolve or a firm determination, the slave is not liable nor punishable for them. Additionally, they will soon vanish, and will not linger in the heart for long.

[2] When someone is infatuated with a woman, for example, and then repents from that, he will at first find the matter to be painful and difficult. But when he patiently endures that pain, keeps himself chaste with regards to this woman, severs every form of interaction between him and her, and lowers his gaze from her, then he is rewarded for that. And this pain will not continue in his heart, by the permission of Allah ﷺ.

[3] Al-Albâni said about it, "Fabricated." See: *Ḍa'eef al-Jâmi' aṣ-Ṣagheer* (5698, 5697) and *as-Silsila aḏ-Ḏa'eefa* (409).

وَأَمَّا مَنْ خَافَ مَقَامَ رَبِّهِ وَنَهَى النَّفْسَ عَنِ الْهَوَى ۞ فَإِنَّ الْجَنَّةَ هِيَ الْمَأْوَى

But as for he who feared the standing of his Lord and prevented the self from [unlawful] whims, then indeed, Paradise will be [his] refuge. [an-Nâzi'ât (79): 40-41]

When the inner-self loves something, it pursues it as best it can, even if that necessitates pursuing a multitude of things that all lead to this end. So whoever exhibits a dispraised love[1], or exhibits a dispraised hatred[2], and does that is sinful. For instance, like when someone hates an individual because of envying him, and then harms those related to him, or withholds their rights, or is hostile towards them. Another example is loving for selfish reasons, and in turn performs the unlawful for them, or performs for selfish reasons what he was commanded to perform for Allah.

These diseases are plentiful within the people, and a person could hate something, and as a result hate many things merely based on illusion and imagination. Likewise, he could love something, and then love many things because of it, also based on illusion and imagination – as the poet said,

Because of loving her, everything black I love,
To the degree that black dogs, because of her, I love.

He had loved a black woman, then subsequently loved black itself, even with regards to dogs. All this sprouts from a disease in the heart that affects its perception and

---

[1] Dispraised love is that which is for other than Allah, and based on whims instead – such as the unlawful *'ishq* of a foreign woman which involves looking, being alone, touching, or committing fornication; may Allah save us from that.

[2] Dispraised hatred is that which is for other than Allah, and for the sake of attaining some worldly gain or its carnal pleasures – such as hating someone for competing with him in a worldly matter, for he wishes to be the sole beneficiary of these pleasures. His hatred in this case is dispraised, in addition to it usually leading to enmity, transgression, and committing injustice against the hated individual and those related to him, such as his family, or children, or students.

will-power, and we ask Allah – the Most High – to relieve our hearts from every disease, and we seek His refuge from the evil *akhlâq*, desires, and diseases.

XII – Returning to Purity

The heart was created solely for loving Allah – the Most High – and this is the *fiṭra* (natural disposition) upon which Allah created His slaves. The Prophet ﷺ said, **"Every child is born upon the *fiṭrah*, then his parents make him into a Jew, Christian, or Fire-Worshipper – just as animals produce wholesome young; do you find in them any flaw?"** Then, Abu Hurayra ﷺ said, "Recite if you wish,

فِطْرَتَ اللَّهِ الَّتِي فَطَرَ النَّاسَ عَلَيْهَا لَا تَبْدِيلَ لِخَلْقِ اللَّهِ

The *fiṭrah* of Allah upon which He has created [all] people. No change should there be in the creation of Allah. [ar-Room (30): 30]

This was collected by al-Bukhâri and Muslim[1].

Allah – the Glorified – disposed His slaves upon loving Him and worshipping Him alone. If this *fiṭra* were left uncorrupted, the heart would be one that knows Allah, loves Him, and worships Him alone. His *fiṭra*, however, becomes corrupted by his disease, such as when his parents make him into a Jew, Christian, or Fire-Worshipper. Even though that was by the will and decree of Allah, these are all [negative] changes to his *fiṭra* upon which He created him[2] – just as a body is changed by amputation – and then could return to the *fiṭra* if Allah ﷻ eases that for the one who strives to restore its *fiṭra*.

---

[1] Narrated by al-Bukhâri (1358) and Muslim (2658).
[2] In other words, Allah ﷻ could sometimes decree matters that are hated to him, for an extensive wisdom. The *fiṭra* being changed from Islam to Judaism, Christianity, or Fire-worship, is an example of that. This is a violation of His Sharia, but takes place by His power and decree for an extensive wisdom.

The Messengers – peace and blessings be upon them – were sent to reinforce this *fitra* and perfect it, not to alter this *fitra* and transform it. And were the heart to love Allah alone, being sincerely devoted to Him in religion, it would not be afflicted with loving other than Him in the first place, nevertheless being afflicted with *'ishq*. Were it to be afflicted with *'ishq*, this is due to a deficiency in its love of Allah alone.

For this reason, since Yoosuf ﷺ loved Allah, and was sincerely devoted to Him in religion, he was not afflicted with that. Rather, the Most High said,

$$كَذَٰلِكَ لِنَصْرِفَ عَنْهُ السُّوءَ وَالْفَحْشَاءَ إِنَّهُ مِنْ عِبَادِنَا الْمُخْلَصِينَ$$

And thus [it was] that We should avert from him evil and immorality. Indeed, he was of Our chosen servants.[1] [Yoosuf (12): 24]

As for the wife of al-'Azeez, she and her people were *mushrik* (polytheist), and thus she was afflicted with *'ishq*.

None is plagued with *'ishq* except due to a deficiency in their *tawheed* and *eemân*. Otherwise, the heart that is attached to Allah, and fears Him, contains two deterrents from *'ishq*: the first being its attachment to Allah and love of Him. That is more delightful and pleasant than everything, and thus loving Allah leaves no room for loving the creation to crowd it [in the heart]. The second is its fear of Allah, for the fear that opposes this *'ishq* dispels it. Anyone who loves something, with or without *'ishq*, is deterred from loving it by loving what is more beloved to him if it crowds it. As well, he is deterred from loving it by fearing a harm that is more hateful to him than dismissing that love. Therefore, when Allah is more beloved to the slave than anything else, and strikes more fear in him than anything else,

---

[1] Shaykh al-Islâm frequently cites this verse as proof using its alternate recitation, *mukhliseen* [instead of *mukhlaseen*]. *Mukhliseen* means those who purified their worship and love of Allah ﷻ, and *mukhlaseen* means those whom Allah purified solely for His worship and enabled them to perform it. Therefore, according to the first recitation (*mukhliseen*), this would be a manifestation of **"Only You we worship,"** [al-Fâtiha (1): 5] while according to the second – more famous – recitation (*mukhlaseen*), this would be a manifestation of **"Only You we ask for help."** [al-Fâtiha (1): 5]

no *'ishq* or crowding will ever take place – except during heedlessness and [instances] when this love and fear weakens, due to abandoning obligations or performing prohibitions. This is because *eemân* increases with acts of obedience, and decreases with sin. So whenever the slave performs an act of obedience out of love for Allah and fear of Him, and refrains from sin out of love for Him and fear of Him – this actually strengthens his love for Him and fear of Him, and in turn removes what the heart contains of loving and fearing other than Him.

This is just like the diseases of the body, wherein its health is preserved by its likes, and the disease is repelled by its opposite. Likewise, the heart that is healthy with *eemân* is preserved by its likes – that which supplies the heart with *eemân*, namely beneficial knowledge and righteous deeds. These are its nourishment, as per the hadith of Ibn Mas'ood that came as both a *marfoo'* and *mawqoof* report, **"Indeed, every *âdib* (host) loves that his banquet is visited, and the banquet of Allah is the Qur'an."**[1]

The *âdib* is the host, so it alludes to Allah hosting those worshipping [Him] in the end of the night, at the times of *âdhân* and *iqâma*, during *sujood* (prostration), and at the end of every *salâh*. Add to this *istighfâr* (seeking forgiveness), for whoever asks forgiveness from Allah and repents to Him, He grants him great satisfaction until an appointed term.

As well, let him adopt a *wird* (routine) of supplications in the daytime and before sleeping, and let him patiently endure whatever impediments and diversions he encounters. Before long, Allah will aid him with a spirit from Him, and will infuse his heart with *eemân*. Let him be keen to perfect the five obligatory prayers, internally and externally, for they make up the firmest column of the religion. Let his motto in life be *lâ hawla wa lâ quwwata illâ billâh* (there is no might or power except by Allah), for through it the weights are carried, the fears are faced, and the lofty stations are attained.

And he must never grow tired of supplicating and requesting, for the slave is responded to unless he says, "I have supplicated, and supplicated, but have received no response." Let him know that victory is with patience, with distress there is relief, with

---

[1] Narrated by al-Bayhaqi in *Shu'ab al-Eemân* (2012). It was deemed weak by al-Albâni in *Da'eef al-Jâmi' as-Sagheer* (4247), and he said in *as-Silsila ad-Da'eefa wal-Mawdoo'a* (2058), "Fabricated."

difficulty there is ease, and that no one ever attained a good end, no Prophet or otherwise, except through patience.

And all praise is for Allah, Lord of the worlds. All praise is for Him for the favor of Islam and the Sunnah – a praise that suits His blessings, which are apparent and hidden, and appropriate for His Noble Face and Honorable Majesty. And may the abundant peace and blessings of Allah be upon our chief, Muhammad, and upon his family, his companions, his wives – the mothers of the believers – and all those who follow them in excellence until the Day of Judgment.

51273620R00052

Made in the USA
Middletown, DE
01 July 2019